AF316604

POLICY ANALYSIS OF MID DAY MEAL PROGRAMME FROM SUPPLY CHAIN MECHANISM

Planning Implementation Digitalisation and Effectiveness

Dr. SANGITA DEY

Acknowledgements

The experience of this journey will always remain with me as most cherished and precious memory. I would like to extend heartfelt gratitude to my supervisor Prof. Veera Gupta for her constant mental and emotional support, guidance and motivation throughout the journey. Many thanks to all the Senior Officials/ Directors/ Principals/ Teachers/Parents/Students of Gujarat and Tamil Nadu for their participation and guidance. A heartfelt thanks and gratitude to my strong pillars of my life to my family and friends for their constant support. Thank you.

CONTENTS

LIST OF TABLES

LIST OF FIGURES

LIST OF ABBREVIATIONS

AMS	Automated Manifest System
BISEG	Bhaskaracharya Institute for Space Applications and Geoinformatics
CDPO	Child Development Project Officer
DoCA	Department of Consumer Affairs, Food and Public Distribution
FCI	Food Cooperative India
FIFO	First in First Out
GCMMC	Gujarat Cooperation Milk Marketing Federation ltd
GPS	Global Positioning System
ICDS	Integrated Child Development Scheme
IFMS	Integrated Finance Management System
IVRS	Interactive Voice Response System
JOT	Just on Time
LPG	Liquefied Petroleum Gas
MILP	Mixed Integer Liner Programming
MIS	Monitoring Information System
NAFED	National Agricultural Cooperative Marketing Federation Of India Ltd.
OPR	Quality Program Report
PPP	Public Private Partnership
PTI	Press Trust India
RESECO	Remote Sensing And Communication Centre"
RO	Reverse Osmosis
SCM	Supply Chain Mechanism
STP	Standard Pressure And Temperature
TNCSC	Tamil Nadu Civil Supplies Corporation
VCA	Value Chain Analysis
VSM	Value Stream Mapping

SUMMARY

In 1995, to support nutrition to primary education, one of the ambitious Mid-Day Meal was launched. The main intention behind launching the program was to enhance the universalisation of primary education by focusing in enrolment/retention/ attendance and at the same time focusing on nutritional status in primary classes. As mentioned by (Centre of Policy Research, 2021), "9.12 crore children were benefitted from MDM scheme through 11.35 lakhs schools during fiscal year 2018-2019" (p.1).

In recent years, ill managed implementation of the scheme was highlighted in several audit /media reports. On July 2013, 23 children died after eating mid-day meal in the school. Forensic report confirmed the presence of toxic insecticide strains in the cooking oil used for preparation of food at the school. (NDTV.com). Various past research work has also identified and highlighted issues related to weak governance, e.g., Sindhu A (2014) reports that Mid-Day Meal Scheme, is still in its primary stage with respect to financial allocation, lack of adequate infrastructure, inadequate monitoring and managing system and poor pay to workers. These governance issues were equally propounded in the work of Prasad, Archana (2013), PAISA (2012), DARPG (2012), CAG (2008), Sinha Dipa (2008). Prasad Archana (2013) also reported that mid-day meal scheme is not yielding results compared to the financial allocation. According to Comptroller and Auditor General CAG report (2008) repeated revision of amendment indicated lack of clarity in the objectives of the scheme following by the MHRD.

This irregularity highlights that there is need for reworking on governance to arrive at effective implementation. There is list of studies on identifying what is happening in the implementation process but very fewer studies mainly focus on why it is happening and what best we can suggest to improve the process. Since there are no implementation guidelines as such through which we can improve the implementation process, therefore, there is a need to systematically analyze different levels of supply chain involved in the MDM scheme. To construct a base for comparison of governance framework, supply chain mechanism was used. But before that it is very important to understand about Supply Chain Mechanism all about. Supply chain is mainly a group of different actions that any organization adopts for better delivery and produce useful product or services. To This term was used in 1985 by 'Michal Porter'. He provided a structure through how to generate benefits and find out the loopholes in the process as well as where we can add value addition or delete some activities that can enhance the process. Supply Chain Techniques Till date different models were developed to enhance the production like value addition supply chain, sustainable supply chain model, supply chain governance model and many more. According to the studies, where there is a demand, involvement of stakeholders, intervention at different levels, value chain analysis is appropriate. This process introduced in 1997 by Hines and Rich. In was mentioned that in India this technique were not been used in any government scheme.

Studies based on Supply Chain Mechanism in recent years Fernie (1995) adopted Supply Chain Machanism in the National Health Service. In fact, it was the first paper of SCM in the service industry. Sampson (2000) explored the customer supplier duality in the service organizations as it pertained to SCM in the service industry. O'Brien and Kenneth (1996) proposed an educational supply chain as a tool for strategic planning in education. Cigolini et al. (2004) explored a framework for SCM based on several service industries including automobile, grocery, computers, book publishing etc.. Habib (2009a) represents the first large scale survey/empirical study that systematically investigated input and output of the university through educational SCM. Sabkota. Ranjita (2015) submitted report on need of Value Chain Analysis for policy implementation in Karnataka. Kadari R, and Roy S.M (2016), discussed how to Strengthening the MDMS through MIS and Interactive Voice Response System (IVRS) while implementing the government scheme in Utter Pradesh. Singh .etal., (2018), submitted dissertation on network Design in Mid Day Meal program in Uttar Pradesh.

By using supply chain mechanism the current study tried to identify the stakeholders involved in the process, historical perspectives and changes that has been taken in past decades, list of activities and the process during implementation, community participation and the risk and challenges that occurs at different level in the implementation process. According to the Committee of Sponsoring Organisation of the Thread way commission (COSO), Risk has been defined as, 'the possibility of event that can occur and adversely affect the objectives of the scheme'. It's a major component of supply chain mechanism. Risk and challenges have been traditionally defined as possibility of danger, loss, injury or other consequences during implementation. It could be defined as: preparedness during natural calamities, public policy and institutional risks, logistical and infrastructure related risks and political risks.

Methodology

The main purpose of the study was to find out internal and external factors influencing supply chain process in terms of policy framework, financial capacity, institutional capacity and coordination, management and accountability structure, design and implementation, community roles and risk and challenges. The study adopted Lean Principals of supply chain mechanism for constructing a base to compare the governance framework. The focus of lean is on providing the best quality within the shortest possible lead time, while minimizing waste throughout the processes (waste being classified as any resource that is not being used properly). Earlier we think that minimizing waste means minimizing inventory, but time, effort and people are also resources to be utilized properly. Analyzing how people are used and time is spent is a critical step in minimizing waste. Qualitative research methods are employed for data collection. Both primary and secondary sources were used for collecting data. Tamil Nadu and Gujarat were selected for the study. Both the state adopted different mechanism for implementation. In firth stage, two districts were selected and from each district two blocks were selected purposively from both the states. Two schools from each block were selected randomly. Per school 1 headmaster, 2 teacher and 10 students were randomly selected. Overall, 16 government / government Aided schools was selected from both the states. In Gujarat, centralized kitchen was observed, and in Tamil Nadu, the decentralized kitchen practices were observed. Total 160 students, 32 teachers, 16 principal from 16 schools from both the states were interviewed during the data collection.

Major findings

By using SCM tools & technique, the study first addressed:

The stakeholder's involvement in MDMS. A mapping exercise was done which helped in identifying their requirement and managing their expectation during the process. The study analyzed all activities/actions that are carried out from national to block level through the SCM perspective. The activities were procurement, transportation & distribution, Warehousing/Storage, processing, preparation of meals, physical resources and quality control. The study identified risk and challenges that has been traditionally defined as possibilities related to danger, loss, injury or other consequences. By identifying the risks and challenges it helped in understanding the conceptualization and implementation of the scheme. Perception and suggestions from the beneficiaries' point of view were covered along with some indicators that can be used for the assessment. In addition, the study also elaborates the transformation in the scheme which took place during the duration in past twenty years. It tries to explain, why the situation demands for a policy, how it is being implemented, a need to keep on modifying the processes and also introduction of new mechanism/factors for effective execution.

1. Importance of Stakeholders Mapping

The study identified internal and external stakeholders through mapping exercise in Mid-day meal Scheme. Mapping helped in identifying various stakeholders at different execution levels as per the established process for their requirement and managing their expectation. Mid-day meal scheme is a government driven program therefore active involvement of internal stakeholders can been seen i.e. government institutions at various levels, however external stakeholders have equally important role in the supply chain for making the program successful and sustainable. The role of the farmer in MDMS has deep impacts. They are the strong pillar of the scheme by supplying grains in subsidize rate to the centre. The study indicates towards the governance framework which has been used by Tamil Nadu (Decentralized kitchen model) is very much closer to tools developed based on Lean principles. The important factor that makes Tamil Nadu framework successful is the involvement/commitment and transparency among critical stakeholders (politicians, administrative officers & community participation). One of the important observations which were shared was whenever election happened and a new political party came in power, they didn't stop the resources or reduced the budget of previous social welfare schemes. In fact they added more budgets and provided more services, resources to those particular ongoing schemes. Social welfare schemes were never hampered in any scenario. The same governance framework was highlighted by Carolyn J.Hill, Laurance E. Lynn Jr. (2005), where author insisted in shifting from hierarchical government toward greater reliance on horizontal, hybridized and associational forms of governance for better outcome.

Frequent monitoring and discussion on the status with Principal Secretariat and among all the stakeholders on 23rd of every month is an important activity/factor to keep check on the scheme. In Tamil Nadu, media is also playing an important role/factor as external stakeholders. In every four months, Principal Secretary share recent development of the program and also want feedbacks regarding further improvement with the community via radio or email.TN is having their own guidelines based on the baseline studies, demographic profile and resources available in the state. The high literacy rate in state has supported in making the scheme successful at grassroot level. It was found that at grassroots level information, communication and education among stakeholders is very strong. Communities are aware about the entitlements and demand constant information on menu for which their children are entitled. This type of involvement of external and internal stakeholders gives strong and sustainable base to the system for better outcome. The same has been discussed by B. Gail Smith. (2008), who insisted that interpersonal trust and working to standards are both important to build more sustained local and many conserved food supply chains. Further suggested that cooperation among food manufacturers, retailers, NGOs, government and farmer organizations is vital in order to raise standards for supply chains and to enable farmers to adopt more sustainable agriculture practices.

By analyzing both mechanisms in Tamil Nadu and Gujarat, (decentralized or centralized kitchen), it was observed that Risk and Challenges exist in both mechanisms. In both states, to ensure transparency and accountability of its operations, risk identification and mitigation is needed. It includes all type of risks, whether internal or external.

2. Need of Risk Identification and Mitigation

To control the risk of malpractices, TN has been following various practices like providing eggs with an Agmark on all school working days. Introduction of GPS tracking system of grains from state to the noon meal centre takes place during transportation. For quality control year marked bags with distinct color are being used to avert adulteration of food grains. It was also observed that a buffer stocks and fund of 45 days was maintained at both TNCSC and in schools to manage any incidents related to natural calamities like (heavy rainfall).

In state of Gujarat, it was found during the study that parent's involvement in MDMS was very less due to lack of awareness about the benefits of the scheme. In rural areas, parents are working in fields and they usually asked their children to sit at home and perform household chores. It was also observed that there is lack of availability of skilled data entry operators and dedicated management information system (MIS) cell at district level. Incomplete information sharing by schools was a major issue reported by the officers.

Once we indentify the list of the risks in supply chain, it is important to prioritize the risks. For example, probability of occurrence of the risks, consequences of the risks and cost and resources required for the mitigation of the risks. Government institutions are large organisations, managing huge resources tend to have larger exposure to risk. Therefore, the need of identifying risk and the process of controlling is necessary to ensure transparency and accountability of its operations.

3. Increase Remuneration and Other Incentives

As per the norms of the central government only one post of cook cum helper is allowed for the strength of 25 beneficiaries and an honorarium of Rs 1000/ is allowed in the sharing pattern of 60:40 between centre and state. But in Tamil Nadu, in order to provide quality, healthy, safe and delicious food for children, three staff have been appointed, namely organizer (Salary Rs 7650-Rs 10,478), Cook (Rs 4380- Rs 5,055), Cook assistant (Rs 3368 -Rs 4380). The other benefits which are provided are such as: Special Monthly Pension, Lumsum payment at the time of retirement, Festival Advance, Pongal Bonus, Hill and Winter Allowance, Special Provident Fund cum Gratuity scheme, Additional Charge allowance to noon meal organizers, Family Benefit Funds, New Health Insurance Scheme, General Provident Fund, Casual Leave, Maternity Leave to noon meal employees, Voluntary Retirement.

The officials reported that getting trained and efficient employees is very difficult; hence the above mentioned benefits are being offered to attract and motivate employees to work. It was observed in Tamil Nadu that better coordination among departments and across schemes was happening for creating better impact. This shows that they have already identified those risks in supply chain and have tried to mitigate those issues at various levels.

4. Regular Assessment of Public Private Partnerships (PPPs)

In India, the increased focus on internal controls in government sector is due to the change and development taking place in the environment in which the Indian Government operates. One of the examples is Public Private Partnerships (PPPs). Several studies have reported that there is a large gap in demand and supply of essential social and economic infrastructure and services. The government is actively promoting Public Private Partnerships in the key infrastructure sectors of transport, power, urban infrastructure, tourism, railways and also in many Flagship programs (such as Mid-Day Meal Scheme) for producing accelerated infrastructure investments and minimizing the infrastructure deficits in the country. Henceforth, increased role of private sector as a partner in developmental and similar programs of government raises a question on the productive use of government funds placed at the disposal of private organizations. In order to provide a fair comprehensive, as well as balanced assessment of such contract/partnerships to the government and public, it is essential to focus on identifying the risks and systematic internal control framework in the formulation and execution of these PPPs.

Government of Gujarat supplies meals by PPPs model in most of the Urban Schools. Under the PPPs model, community participation is very less, government role is only limited to monitoring the status of financial transaction and state is totally dependent on the agencies that prepare and supply meals, in this scenario, probability of risk is very high. It is important to control the utilization of funds, the quality and quantity of meal provided to the children. In Gujarat more than 100 contractual cook lost their job due to implementation of centralized mechanism. Wastage of meals was found in schools in Gujarat. Though, Akshaypatra Foundation prepares hygienic meal, the taste was missing as reported by students. Students complained of missing the local taste and hence wasted meal. In eastern part of Ahmedabad where Sri Shakti organization is assigned for meal services, hygiene was a major concern reported. It was reported that the ingredients used for preparation of meals were not of good quality. Most of the student didn't eat meals and visited outside the campus to eat from road side hawkers. During lunch either they eat local snacks or chips. It was felt that Gujarat government is only concerned about the number of meals served and stats like how many children are present, how many of them eat meals. Government was not monitoring the portion of meals students are consuming. In one of the selected sample school 2 - 3 girls were sitting together and sharing food from common plate which appeared as a common practice their for teachers.

In Gujarat, 1.45 lakh children under the age six were suffering from the worst category of malnutrition, i.e. Severe Acute Malnutrition (SAM) and 5.13 Lakhs School going children are suffering from malnourishment and anemia (dnai.in, 2015). There is health related risk that needs to be mitigated. Not only numbers of stats but improvement in nutrition status is required for the development of the nation. We can't say Mid-Day Meal scheme is successful by just achieving only one objective.

5. Awareness Level should be same among all the Stakeholders

Program effectiveness is bound to increase if similar level of understanding can be established among all the stakeholders whether internal or external. When there is a demand, required supply is provided. For e.g. in Tamil Nadu, parents knew that their children will get eggs on daily basis under the provisions of the scheme; hence they made sure during supervision that children are receiving it with meals. For promoting awareness among community and increasing its participation the state government should organized Awareness Generation Mela/ events at different levels.

6. Community Participation through Capacity Building Training Program

This study strongly recommends that community participation is vital to ensure schemes success. There are many issues that can be easily rectified at local level by involving community such as replacement of vessels, sitting mat, maintenance of hygienic environment in the school premises, supply of food on social occasion, community kitchen etc. Just like centralized kitchen in urban area, community kitchen can be innovated in rural areas.

7. Focus on Quantity, Quality and Time

1. Packaging

During field visit to Tamil Nadu, it was observed that superior quality (BOPP) of packaging material is being used for preserving the grains to maintain the quality of grains throughout the season and also there are less chances of leakage either during transportation or storage. BOPP bags are better than gunny bags, they are superior in strength, are moisture resistance and rodents can't easily damage the grains which reduces probability of leakage.

2. Uses of Technology

By using technology and techniques at different levels, Tamil Nadu has controlled malpractices up to some extent. It assures the quality as well as quantity of grains from first to last level. For example, using of weighing machine during loading and unloading at school level, use of GPS tracker, use of stamp on bags as well as on eggs etc.

3. Storage

It is very important to disinfect the room/ place where grains are kept. It should be spacious with proper ventilation and lighting in the room. In past it was seen that rodents as well as pests create problems and hampered the quality of grains. Henceforth regular cleaning and pest control should be done in regular interval.

4. Storing period of grains in go-down

It is very important to analyse the period of storing grains in go-down. The maximum time duration where food grains are kept during overall supply chain is in go-down, which may affect the quality of grains. It is very important to assure how the grain has been kept at what condition.

5. Monitoring and Supervision

It should be done digitally at all levels as it will reduce time, cost and manpower. During study it was observed that at all level documentation was consuming too much time. Keeping records was a big challenge. Officials who visited schools and fill the assigned formats reported that they don't have time to enter the data again in computer. It consumes their working time.

6. Cooking and Serving Mechanism

Training of cooks on food safety and on techniques of cooking to keep nutrition intact is an important activity. Precautionary action needs to be taken while preparation by using fresh water, air tight container should be used for storage of grains. Plastic container or spoon should be avoided.

7. Time taken for preparation of food

To maintained the nutrition value it is very important to study the time taken for preparation of food and also the time taken to reach the beneficiaries. In case of centralized kitchen, meals are cooked in the early hour of the day, till the time it get served, it doesn't remain enough warm as a result children were observed wasting food is one of the key observation.

8. Ingredients used in preparation

It has been noticed that states are mostly using palm oil for cooking. There are studies that explain about the harms of palm oil. The only reason for use of palm oil could be its cost effectiveness compared to other oils. The salt and other spices should be of Agmark certification. Agmark is a certified mark employed on agricultural products in India, assuring that they confirm to a set of standards approved by the Directorate of marketing and inspection office of the Department of Agriculture.

9. Hygiene practices

The cleanliness must be maintained throughout the entire supply chain/activities either at go-down, school storage, kitchen, while cooking and also among children. Not only that, drinking facilities, area where children sit and eat, the person who served food (whether they are following hygiene practices by using caps and gloves etc) need to be assure.

10. Waste of food by children

Teacher and parents who supervise should notice whether children are consuming sufficient quantity of meal or not. If children are wasting meals, they should be asked about the reason behind the act. It was noticed in Gujarat, where centralized mechanism is working successfully, wastage of meals by children is very common. Children revealed that though they are getting different variety of meal every day, the taste is missing.

11. Information Flow

As soon as orders are placed for food grains the time taken towards its release determines the overall time it will take to reach at different destinations in the entire supply chain. This could also be applied in releasing fund. As soon as the fund get released, processing start to allocate grains and forward the same for the next level. In both the situation time is crucial.

12. Transparency in selection of third party

The contract for selection of third party should mention each and every protocol that needs to be followed. The contractor selection should be based on their previous performance and preferably belonging to the local demographic region.

13. Coordination of all the activities

This is the one of the most important element of any supply chain. For the effective delivery of services, the process of reporting, storage, fund transformation, flow of information, uses of techniques and coordination among all the actors should be synced at program implementation level.

Conclusion

Every step involved in supply chain need to be analysed for maximum utilization of available resources for sustaining the program. Currently the traditional practice of analyzing the scheme is not at all sufficient. There is huge scope for further studies on the same issues as very limited research work is available. The current study will help to construct a basic understanding of scheme through Supply Chain Management perspective and its significance.

Digital Platform (Web and Mobile Application Based) For Facilitating MDMS

The study is proposing a digital framework in Mid-day Meal Scheme through designing and implementing Electronic Mid-day Meal Network (eMDMN), an innovation that will bring together technology, people and processes to strengthen the mid-day meal supply chain by digitizing information on at all levels.

Figure: The Three integral parts of eMDMN

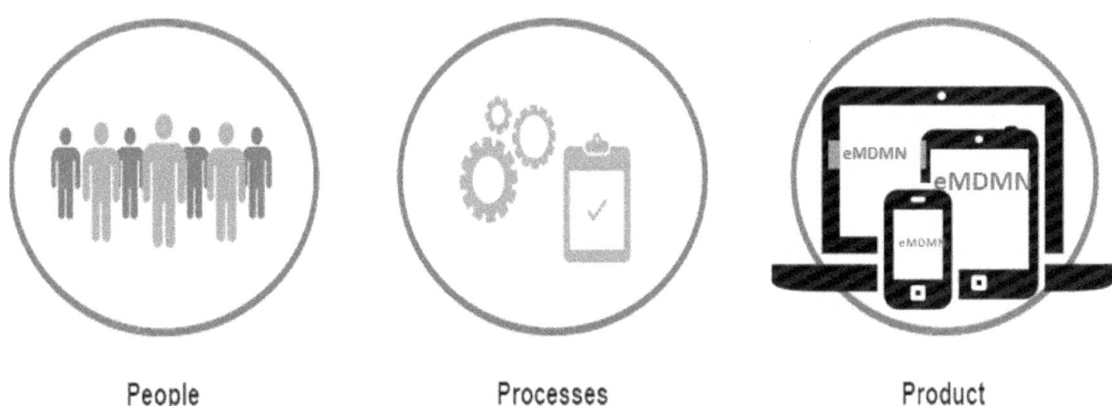

What is eMDMN?

An electronic supply chain management information system (eSCMIS) that will use Web interface/Smartphone, and IoT device with cloud-based technology to capture real-time data across the entire supply chain, from the FCI godown to the last-mile school.

Its aim will be to streamline and regularize the food grains flow network by ensuring data-driven and efficient management of the supply chain. eMDMN will help in capturing data at all levels of supply chain digitally. A mobile application can be used by all internal stake holders who are directly implementing the scheme e.g. officials of district and block level, Head master, teachers, parents, cooks etc. For external and indirect persons involved in implementation, web based interface will be helpful e.g. District collector, Food commissioner, agencies like FCI, transporters etc. Facilitating real-time monitoring of flow of goods and services through mobile based digital application and web interface will be an advantage for the scheme. Once the technology is ready a pilot can be done in some parts of country with selecting different geographic and demographic location. Later working on building capacity of all government and private personnel for supply chain management on (eMDMN) will be required for its nationwide implementation.

CHAPTER I

INTRODUCTION

This chapter provides the background information of Mid Day Meal Scheme in India. It discussed the implementation issues occurring in the country from past many years and highlights the need of conducting the study.

1.1 BACKGROUND OF THE STUDY

Education is the base of modernisation and human development; it cuts across three dimensions economic, cultural and political, which are considered the measuring roots of development process (Sikligar, 2010). It makes people skilled towards jobs and creates productive efficiency. Now a days, the development of the nation hinges-on its capacity to acquire, adapt and then to advance knowledge. This capacity largely depends upon the extent to which the county's population has attained literacy, numeracy, communication and problem solving skills.

According to the study, India's GDP was 7.2 percent in 2017-18 and 7 percent in 2018-19. India's labour force is expected to touch 160-170 million by 2020. The major factor behind this projection is based on population growth, increased labour force participation, and higher education enrolment. Therefore, to promote education, government of India grants financial assistance and loan to the states and union territories for different tasks like (1) opening and maintenance of Ashram schools (2) hostel facilities (3) organizing and development teaching materials (4) stipends for primary and higher education (5) supplying reading and writing materials (6) dress and uniform for students (7) exempting scheduled caste and scheduled tribes candidates from tuition fees (8) pre and post scholarship and (9) making arrangement of mid day meals to the students.

1.2 MID DAY MEAL SCHEME

In 1995, to support nutrition to primary education, one of the ambitious Mid Day Meal was launched. The main intention behind launching the program was to enhance the universalisation of primary education by focusing in enrollment/retention/attendance and at the same time focusing on nutritional status in primary classes. Across the world, Mid Day Meal scheme is known as School Feeding Programme (SFP). It has been seen as a social safety net for vulnerable sections of the population and as an educational intervention. By ensuring that children visit schools and their learning is improved by elimination of hunger in the class room.

Figure 1: Beneficiaries of MDMS

On the other hand, as we all know that malnutrition not merely gives rise to morbidity and mortality, it also prevents a child from developing into a fully functional adult. Malnutrition on a very serious note can adversely affects universalisation of Elementary Education (UEE) in the following ways: if the child is not keeping well, their energy is low; there is less chance of them to participate in school activities and concentrate on study. According to the World Bank, ground report on Malnutrition, "it was estimated that India is one of the highest ranking countries in the world for the number of children suffering from malnutrition," 2013. The 2017 Global Hunger Index & International Food Policy Research Institute (IFPRI) ranked India 100th out of 118 countries with a serious situation. In year 2018, India stood 103 out of 119 countries with a serious issue of child wasting. According to W.H.O report, "at least one in every 5 children under the age of 5 years in India suffers from wasting. Children, therefore tend to dropout, *inter alia,* inability to cope, even if the child does not actually dropout, their attainment levels tend to be low,"2015. Under such circumstances, Mid Day Meal Scheme can play an effective role in minimizing malnutrition as well as in achieving Universalisation of Elementary Education (UEE).

1.3 DEVELOPMENT OF MID DAY MEAL SCHEME

On 15 August 1995, The National Programme of Nutritional Support to Primary Education (NSPE) popularly known as MDM was launched. According to the MHRD repot ("The scheme was launched in 2408 blocks across the country for providing one meal per day to student in primary school (class 1 to 5). It was later made universal by extending the coverage to all government and government schools in 2001, following the Supreme Court order dated November 28 of the same year. The scope of the scheme was further extended to cover the students of upper primary (class VI to VIII) in 2007.In addition this program was supported by Right to Education Act, 2009 which mandated the provision of a kitchen in every school, where Mid Day Meal can be cooked. Later the scheme was strengthened by the National Food Security Act, in 2013 which laid down the legal entitlement of every school children to provide free hot cooked meal to children upto 14 years",2017).

Figure 2: Timeline of Mid Day Meal Scheme

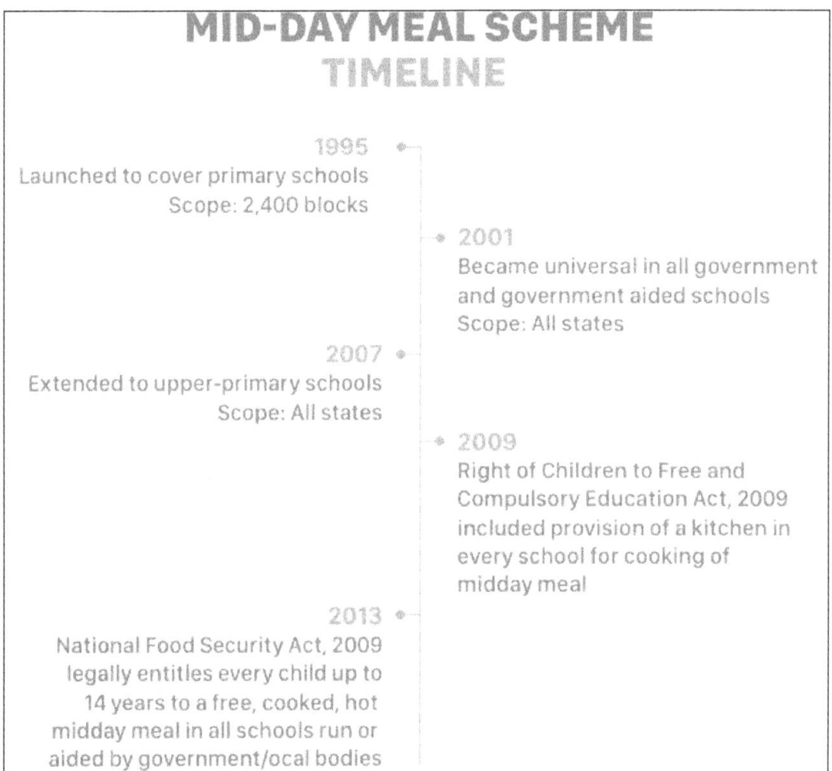

Source: MHRD

1.4 COVERAGE OF MID DAY MEAL SCHEME

According to MHRD, "the cooking cost per child per day is Rs.4.48 for primary and Rs 6.71 for upper primary children. To deliver MDM at this rate, in most states the centre contributes 60 percent while the state share; is 40 percent. In the northeast states, the contribution of the centre is 90 percent and the respective state is 10 percent and the scheme is funded 100 percent by the central government in all union territories'. According to MHRD data, "11.98 crore children are enrolled in the primary and upper primary schools (from 1 to VIII) in the country in government schools and government aided schools. Out of the total children enrolled, only about 76.5 percent (9.17 crore) children benefitted under the MDM scheme as on March 31, 2019. However, the MDMs approved by the government was for a total of 9.58 crore children,"2019.

Figure 3: Coverage of Mid Day Meal in India

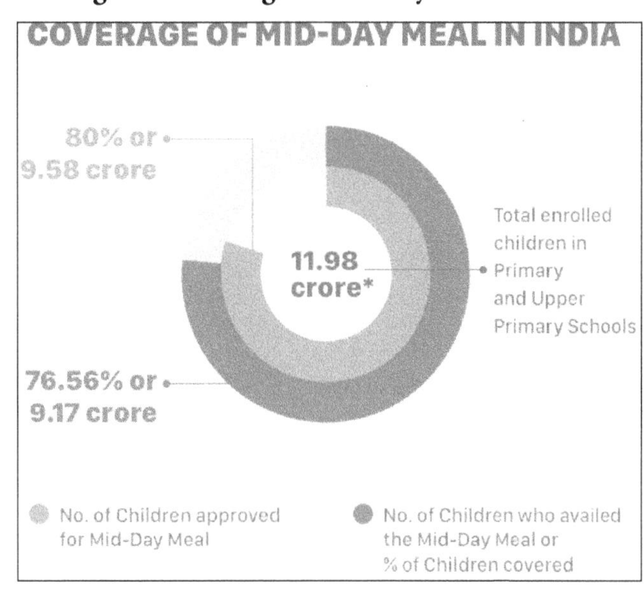

Source: MHRD

1.5 NUTRITION VALUE AND NORMS UNDER MID DAY MEAL SCHEME

According to the prescribed guidelines by MDMS (2012), ("the children studying in primary school must be provided with at least 450 calories with 12 of protein, where as the children from upper primary school should get 700 calories with 20 grams of protein. Further, the food intake per meal by children of primary classes, as mentioned in guidelines by MHRD is 100 grams of food grain, 20 grams of pulses, 50 grams of vegetables and 5 grams of oils and fats. For the children of upper –primary schools, the mandated breakup is 150 grams of food grains of pulses, 75 grams of vegetables and 7.5 grams of oils and fat." There are literature that highlighted "providing free and nutritious meals during the school day, MDM program has shown significant increase in intake of daily calorie and level of protein and iron among recipient children," (Afridi,2007). There are list of literature who pointed that there was increase in enrolment in all classes year on year basis. There was a big jump in enrolment at all levels in both the

Figure 4: Food Norms under MDM

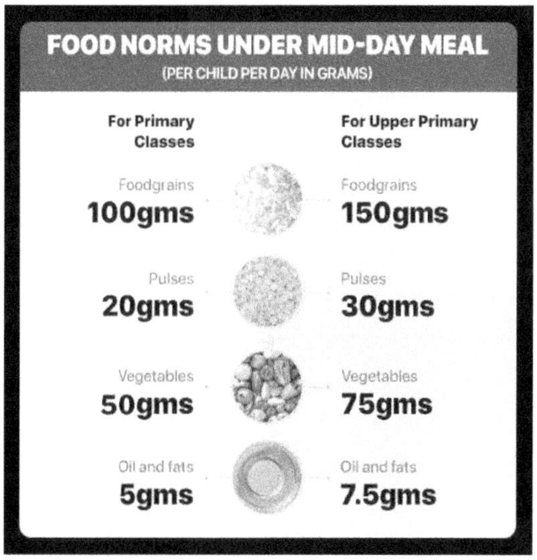

Source: MHRD

periods it was evident that the rate of increase in enrolment during the cooked meal scheme (3.8 % per annum) has been much higher compared to the rate of growth of enrolment when the dry ration scheme 1.5 % per annum) was in operation (Rani.Anima and Sharma Naresh.K(2008).

Figure 5: Weekly Menu under Social Welfare and Nutritious Meal Program under Government of Tamil Nadu

Days	Images	1st and 3rd week Menu	Images	2nd and 4th week Menu
Monday	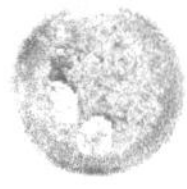	Vegetable Briyani + Pepper Egg	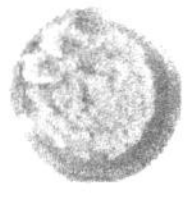	Sambar Sadham (Bisibelabath) + Onion Tomato Masala Egg
Tuesday	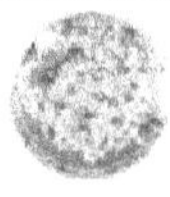	Black gram pulav + Tomato Masala Egg	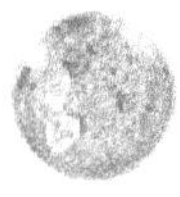	Mixed Meal Maker & Vegetables Rice + Pepper Egg
Wednesday		Tomato Rice + Pepper Egg		Tamarind Rice + Tomato Masala Egg
Thursday		Rice + Sambar+Boiled Egg	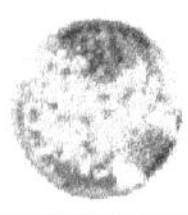	Lemon Rice + Sundal + Tomato Egg
Friday	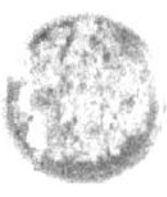	Curry Leaf Rice / Keerai Sadham + Masala Egg & Chilly Fried Potato	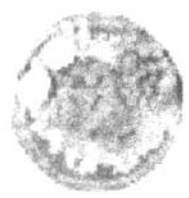	Rice + Sambar + Boiled Egg and Fried Potato

This is one of the best practices in Tamil Nadu, where they have almost 10 healthy meal options that are provided to our growing children. Meal is complete combination of carbohydrates, fiber, protein, fats and other minerals that is needed on daily basis. According to (MHRD, 2019) "some states like Andhra Pradesh, Maharashtra and West Bengal are performing much better that highly populated states. In Andhra Pradesh, 82 percent of children are availing MDM. The state provides eggs/banana to children twice a week using the state own resources. Maharashtra with 82 percent of MDM coverage has a unique practice of serving ' snehbhojan'(special treats which comprises sweet and snacks) to children on occasion of birthdays of eminent people of the state".

1.6 COVERAGE OF MID DAY MEAL SCHEME IN STATE WITH LITERACY RATE HIGHER THAN NATIONAL LITERACY RATE

"All the states where literacy rate is higher than national rate of 74 percent have shown a good performance under Mid Day Meal scheme. For example, Kerala, the state with the highest literacy rate is also among the best performing states under the MDM scheme. The state provided additional food items like eggs/ banana once a week and 150 milliliters of milk twice a week to each student. The state has recently announced that it will be adding 1 fruit per day with its regular meals. Mizoram that has the second –highest literacy rate in the country serves mid day meals to 92 percent of its enrolled children. The state encourages schools to grow vegetables within the school compound because of which most schools in rural areas have their own kitchen gardens. Similarly, Goa and Himachal Pradesh, where the MDM coverage is 87.5 percent and 91 percent respectively, are performing better than many other states in the country in terms of efficient fund usage, food quality and infrastructure"(MHRD,2019).

Figure 6: Coverage of MDMS with Literacy Rate

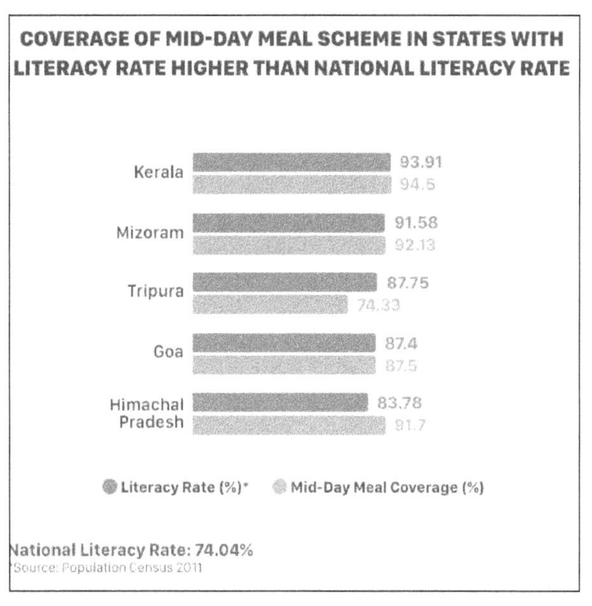

1.7 COVERAGE OF MID DAY MEAL WITH HIGH POPULATION

'In Uttar Pradesh almost one forth (4.3 crore) of its 20 crore people are aged between 5 and 14 years according to Population Census 2011, making it the state of highest child population in country. UP has about 1.8 crore children enrolled for MDM in 1.5 Lakh primary and middle schools. The state has time and again made to the headlines for irregularities and corruption in the Implementation of MDM. MHRD highlighted that in last 3 years UP has maximum number of complaints (14) against corruption to implementation of MDM. Total of 154 children were reported ill as reported by MHRD. On the other hand, Kerala with 94.5 percent coverage, Assam with 95.02 percent, West Bengal 94.06 percent and Nagaland with 96.89 percent are best performing states, (MHRD 2019).

Figure 7: Coverage of MDMS in states with high population

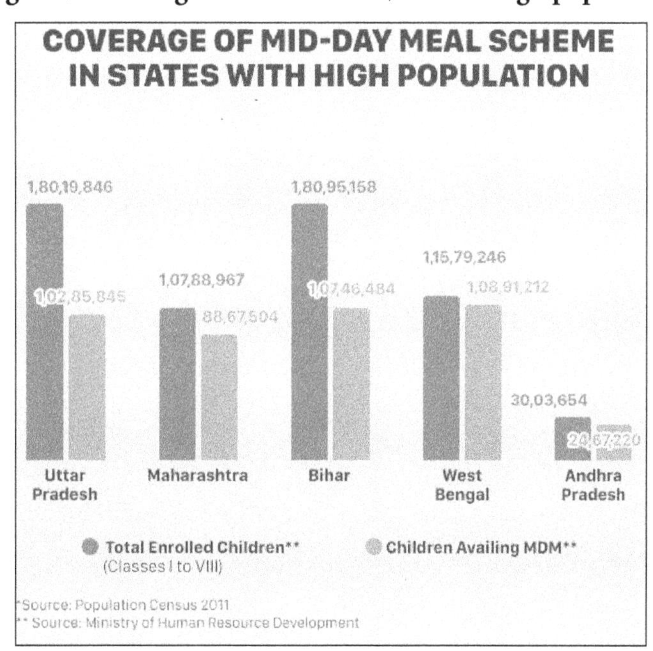

Source: MHRD

1.8 IMPLEMENTATION ISSUES IN MID DAY MEAL SCHEME

In recent years, ill managed implementation of the scheme was highlighted in several audit /media reports. "On July 2013, 23 children died after eating mid day meal in the school. Forensic report confirmed the presence of toxic insecticide strains in the cooking oil used for preparation of food at the school" (NDTV.com). According to the data provided in Annual Work Plan and Budget Reports of MDM by the Ministry of Ministry of Human Resource Development, among all the states in the country, Uttar Pradesh (UP), Bihar, and Jharkhand are the worst performing states with mid day meal coverage of 57.8 percent, 59.39 percent and 61. 45 percent.

Various past research work has identified and highlighted issues related to weak governance, e.g., "Mid Day Meal Scheme, is still in its primary stage with respect to financial allocation, lack of adequate infrastructure, inadequate monitoring and managing system and poor pay to workers"(Sindhu, 2014, p.11). These governance issues was equally propounded in the work of Prasad, Archana (2013), PAISA (2012), DARPG[1] (2012),CAG[2] (2008), R,Rukmani (2011) Sinha,Dipa (2008). Prasad, Archana (2013) also reported that mid day meal scheme is not yielding results compared to the financial allocation. According to Comptroller and Auditor General, India (CAG,2008), ("repeated revision of amendment indicated lack of clarity in the objectives of the scheme following by the MHRD who is not following the prescribed guidelines"). Some of the issues linked with implementation of the scheme have been highlighted by the MHRD which were based on progress reports submitted by the states in the year 2012. They have been mentioned in following table:

Table 1: Key issues linked with implementation of the scheme

Issues	State(s) where these problems were reported
Irregularity in serving meals	Karnataka, Madhya Pradesh, Orissa, Rajasthan, Maharashtra, Arunachal Pradesh
Irregularity in supply of food grains to schools	Orissa, Maharashtra, Tripura, Karnataka, Arunachal Pradesh, Meghalaya, Delhi, Andhra Pradesh
Caste based discrimination in serving of food	Orissa, Rajasthan, Madhya Pradesh
Poor quality of food	Rajasthan, Tamil Nadu, Delhi, Chhattisgarh
Poor coverage under School Health Programme	Orissa, Jharkhand, Madhya Pradesh, Rajasthan, Uttar Pradesh, Manipur, Arunachal Pradesh, Himachal Pradesh, Chhattisgarh
Poor infrastructure (kitchen sheds in particular)	Andhra Pradesh, Tamil Nadu, Puducherry, Gujarat, Chandigarh, Himachal Pradesh, Jammu and Kashmir, Orissa
Poor hygiene	Delhi, Rajasthan, Puducherry,
Poor community participation	Most states – Delhi, Jharkhand, Manipur, Andhra Pradesh in particular

Source: Ministry of Human Resource Development-2012

Out of many governance issues, financial allocation is one of the major one, as the cooking cost is the major concern among all the financial issues. Different studies pointed that central assistance to meet cooking cost

---

1. Department of Administrative Reforms and Public Grievances (DAR&PG)

2. Comptroller and Auditor General, India (CAG) (2008)

is much lower than the actual requirement (The Planning Commission Working Group, 2010), (CAG,"Audit report on MDM" 2008), (R Rukmani, 2011) (DARPG,2012). Different studies also highlighted that the under financing also impacted on the utensils and material used in the preparation of meal. (PAISA 2012)[3], (Prasad, Archana 2013), (R Rukmani, 2011), (Sinha Dipa, 2008). At this stage it is important to understand the meaning of Governance perspective as it refers to the process and structure used to direct and manage an organisations operation and activities. It defines the division of power and establishes the mechanisms to achieve accountability between owners, manager and stakeholders and the entities that is the organization. Governance helps the organisation focus on the activities and to utilize their resources effectively and ensure that they are managed in the best interests of their principal stakeholders (.Manus.Mc, 2008).

Lack of defined structure for implementation cripples the pace of coverage for any programme and creates hurdles in delivering services (Economic Times (2013). The same has been supported by Planning Commission (2010) stated that states did not follow the guidelines of Government of India to deliver food grains at the school by PDS dealer, thereby allowing the leakage of food grains which as a result, impedes the entire food grains flow management.

A CAG (2008)report pointed towards projected enrolments by states on basis of which food grain disbursements are made, were unrealistically high compared to historical and actual enrolment. There have been several instances of mismatch in utilisation of cooking costs and food grains procured by states. According to CAG (2008), none of the states were able to furnish utilisation certificates nor had they identified ways to reduce theft and misuse of food grains. In addition, PAISA (2012A) report revealed that records to monitor food grain flow were poorly maintained. Inconsistencies were found in data recorded among different monitoring reports and account books. The reports also revealed that district administration does not have a fixed mechanism to monitor lifting food grains by the school. A similar finding has been reported in study done by (DARPG 2012), and Sinha,Dipa (2008).According to the report on Budget briefs on MDM Scheme 2020-2021 Accountability Research, Centre for Policy Research, there are differences in enrollment figure as given in Unified District Information System for education (U-DISE) and those in the PAB. That indicates governance issues at centre level.

When examined about the quality of monitoring at grassroots level, deviation from prescribed norms came into light and revealed that many states do not monitor the quality of food prepared at schools levels CAG (2008). Loopholes in monitoring were also reported in number of studies CAG (2008), PAISA (2012A), Sinha,Dipa (2008). In addition, various gaps related to implementation which included community involvement, health & safety and capacity building has been highlighted in the studies DARG (2012), Prasad, Archana (2013), PAISA (2012).

Nowadays a big debate on opting for centralize versus decentralize kitchen practices in states is taking place. The union government had proposed centralize kitchen practices in the year 2004, wherein a state had option to shift from decentralize kitchen to centralize if they faced any implementation challenges. But what studies have suggested that the centralized practices have also suffering due to ill management. Few examples are lack in providing nutritional food; less community involvement, tasteless food, and late arrival time of meal at school were some of the major issues highlighted in past studies. DARG (2012),CMDM) PEO(2010), Sinha,Dipa (2008). Furthermore,in more than twenty years how the transformation of scheme took place is discussed in Chapter IV Policy Framework of MDMS.

---

3. Planning, Allocations and Expenditures, Institutions: Studies in Accountability(PAISA)

1.9 RATIONAL OF THE STUDY

Henceforth, list of literature reflect that the scheme suffers from structural problems; the biggest of them is inadequate monitoring mechanism and lack of accountability. Reviews suggested that there is a substantial gap in implementing the prescribed guidelines of the scheme. Deviation from norms in terms of financial allocation, food grains, process of implementation, monitoring mechanism and standard of meals provided to the beneficiaries are reported. This irregularity highlights that there is need for rework on governance to arrive at effective implementation. There are list of studies on identifying what is happening in the implementation process but very less studies mainly focus on why it is happening and what best we can suggest to improve the process. Despite investing large amount of funds and resources, as a tax payer, we are accountable to know that why are we not able to achieve desired target? Why the scheme is ill managed after taking multiple measures? How poor quality of food grains reached the schools from FCI, when there is a set list of protocols to maintain it? What is the storage condition? In case of any incident, are schools and their staffs should be held responsible? Why guidelines on best practices made at centre level are not penetrating till grassroots level? Is there lack in coordination between sectors and actors involved? Or the officials involved in MDM are not receiving adequate support to analyze the situation? Or they are overloaded with other program responsibilities? There is list of queries which indicate whom to blame and avoid in this governance. Henceforth there is a need to study from the perspective of supply chain mechanism since there are no implementation guidelines as such through which we can improve the implementation process.

In previous decade, there are studies focusing on issues at ground e.g. school management committee, quality of kitchen or selection of food varieties, quality of food, and nutrition. Similarly there are studies that were conducted targeting on top functions of the scheme e.g. policy implementation, fund release, monitoring mechanism, decentralization of authority etc. However very few of them have focused on the supply chain e.g. where the food grains come from, its transportation and condition and timelines till it reaches to the beneficiaries. What technologies are being used to control malpractices? How is the selection of third party done etc? The issues may not be only within the ground or at top level. Within these levels, there are levels where number of stakeholders gets involved. A list of internal and external factors involved in the process need to be identified and studied to avoid mismanagement, and improve effectiveness of the scheme. Hence there is a need to systematically analyze different levels of supply chain involved in MDM scheme. It will help us to understand each and every process, identify steps/processes that can be removed, and addition of steps to make the process effective and efficient.

CHAPTER II

REVIEW OF LITERATURE

This chapter examines some of the published research work, journals, books, documents, reports and articles related to public policy planning & process, mid-day meal scheme practices & challenges in implementation, implementation framework, supply chain mechanism etc. An attempt has been made to put together a collection of brief summary of previous research findings and writings of recognised experts. The literatures has been categorised into different themes:

2.1 BENEFITS OF MDMS ON EDUCATION

Rani, A and Sharma, N. (2008) conducted 'An Empirical study of the MDM Programe in Khurda, Orissa on enrolment data for nine years from 1995-96 to 2003-04 for 10 schools, where the period involves implementation of both types of the schemes under the MDMS(cooked meal and fry rations)-cooked meals scheme from 1995-96 to 2000-01 and dry rations scheme from 2000-01 to 2003-04. The authors have pointed that there was increase in enrolment in all classes on every year basis. There was a big jump in enrolment at all levels in both the periods it was evident that the rate of increase in enrolment during the cooked meal scheme (3.8 % per annum) has been much higher compared to the rate of growth of enrolment when the dry ration scheme 1.5 % per annum) was in operation. Though this study highlighted that there is increase in enrollment but was not discussed about children's physical and mental development, as well as their participation in education.

Pratichi trust (2005) conducted a study in Birbhum district of west Bengal, observed in its evaluation of MDMS that scheme had led to a significant increase in enrolment and attendance of children. The increase is particularly highlighted in girls and children from the schedule caste and schedule tribes. It also observed that the MDMS has averted severe under-nourishment, reduced social distance and curbed teacher absenteeism.

Jain and Shah (2005) conducted a survey in 70 'most backward' villages of Madhya Pradesh reported that 90 % of teachers and cooks responded that meal is regularly provided, and that 96 % of parents want to be continued. Also, 63 % of parents and 74 % of teachers felt that the meals have improved child learning abilities. Overall enrolment increased around 15%. Enrollment is higher in the caseof SC/ST (43%), girls (38%), and SC/ST(41%).

Jayaraman,et.a,l(2004) using panel data of 500,000 schools in 15 major states across India observed annually from 2002 to 2004, that MDMS result in substantial increases in primary school enrolment, driven by early primary school responses to the program. In an extension, using cross-sectional household and school survey data from the Indian Human Development Survey (IHDS) 2005, they provided suggestive evidence that the positive enrolment response associated with MDM is not accompanied by improved learning, as measured by test scores for reading, writing and mathematics among 8-11 year-olds. This suggested that MDMS, although were effective at encouraging early school enrolment but are less effective at retaining students or encouraging their re-enrolment in upper primary school.

Dreze and Vivek (2002) in their survey of 26 villages in Sikar district (Rajasthan) found that school enrolment had sharply raised after mid-day meals were introduced, with an average increase of 25 %. They reported that in some 'alternative schools' located in deprived hamlets, enrolment nearly doubled after the introduction of mid-day meals.

2.2 BENEFITS OF MDMS ON HEALTH

Afridi (2007) mentioned that by providing free and nutritious meals during the school day, India's MDM program has shown significant increase in intake of daily calorie and level of protein and iron among recipient children.

Ramachandran. et,a.l (2000) emphasized that the children were assured of their name being registered in schools as a proof of their official enrolment due to implementation of the MDM scheme. However this by itself does not ensured their regular attendance in the school. This emphasizes the role and responsibilities of the community, SMC, PTA and other internal stakeholders to monitor and identify what all is needed to fill the gap and make more interesting so that children not only focus on meal but also study.

2.3 PRACTICES OF MDMS

5th Joint Review Mission on MDM scheme Tamil Nadu (MHRD report 2014) the state government is providing egg to all the elementary age children on all working days (five days). The 633193 children of 9th and 10th Class were also provided MDM by the state government from its own resources. Variety of rice scheme has been introduced by Chief Minister of TN with effect of 20th march, 2013. Every month requirement of Pulses and salt are delivered at school by TNCSC between 15th to 25th of the previous month, so that each school has buffer stock as per MDM guidelines. One Noon Meal Organiser, 1 cook, 1 assistant cook are engaged in each school for ensuring uninterrupted preparation and serving of MDM in all schools.

MHRD (2014) The Tamil Nadu State Government not only made sufficient budget provision for constant supply of food items and infrastructure facilities, but increased budget provisions which are made every year for continuous improvement in the management systems and quality of food delivered. TNCSC ensures constant supply of food items. At the institutional level, preparation and distribution of MDM is a team effort which includes not only the regular workers but also the member of the village education committee.

Shanmugam,R. et.al (2012) highlighted that the state of Tamil Nadu has implemented best practices that could be replicated in other states. They supply double fortified with Vitamin A and iodine under MDM scheme in Goitre prone 7 districts. Due to its effectiveness in eradication of Goitre, it has been extended to all schools in the state. Second is inclusion of egg, 3 times a week for covering higher protein requirement of the children. For internal monitoring of the program, involvement of Panchayati Raj Institutions is included in the village level committee in TN.

Athreya,V.B (2011) discussed about the process of implementation of MDM program in Tamil Nadu. It emphasis that most of the program go through a process of evolution before they become embedded in the policy framework. Secondly, sustained political will and the virtues of active political competition in a pluralist democracy where the poor are underrepresented in most public spaces and forums. The author mentioned that, the scheme contributes a valuable investment in form of human development and country's future forthe benefited children in the age group of (2 to 15 years). It is also a partial fulfillment of states' responsibilities towards children, both in terms of international covenants to which India is a signatory and in terms of the constitutional mandate of ensuring the right to life which includes the right to food as mandated by Supreme

Court of India. Further suggested that there are areas, where improvement is needed. Involvement of elected local bodies is needed.

Menon,P. (2009) pointed in her evaluation report that MDM program seems to enjoy all round support from the village community. Even teachers, who tend to have various reservations in other states, strongly support the program. With sound arranging in place, the MDM doesn't interfere with their teaching duties and most of the teachers met during the study has appreciation of the positive aspects of school lunches. Finally, concluded that Tamil Nadu's experience suggests that well devised school meals have much to contribute to the advancement of elementary education, child nutrition and social equity.

Dasmunshi, P(2008) mentioned in his report that under MDMS in Tamil Nadu, it was decided to empower mothers of 12 crore school going children covered under the scheme to supervise the preparation and serving of the meal. Mother is being encouraged to come forward and take turn to supervise the feeding of the children. Thus, ensuring regularity and quality of the meal. This initiative was aimed to give mothers a voice and a role fortaking ownership of the program. Therefore the States has been requested to launch a concentrated campaign towards mass mobilization of mothers at grassroot level. It is suggested that at this stage the Government can take NGOs support for this nobel initiative.

Public Private Partnership for implementing MDMS (2010) after investing many implementation issues, on the basis of The Planning Commission recommendationin 2010, the Plan Panel has suggested that Public private partnership will ensure better delivery of services and therefore a better performance of the scheme. Launched in 2005, the school meal program is one of the most successful programs of govt. of India. It aims to protect children from classroom hunger, increase school enrollment and attendance, check malnutrition and empower underprivileged section of society. Experts too supported the planning commission's recommendation on PPP mode as one of the best models for the better service and performance of the scheme. According to D. Jagannath Rao, former bureaucrat and renowned educationalist who authored a book on Elementary Education in India: Status, Issues and Concern argues that the Akshaya Patra Program bear as eloquent testimony to the efficiency of successful collaborative effort between governments and the foundation. The inherent strength that Akshya Patra stresses is that willingness to work in remote areas, ability to set in motion a participatory process in identification of the needs, the design and implementation of the scheme, the readiness to mobilized and use local resources, effective service delivery and freedom to innovate.

2.4 CHALLENGES IN IMPLEMENTATION OF MDM

Sindhu, A (2014A) illustrated that, India's prestigious flagship program national Program for MDM meals in schools, is still in its primary stage with constraints of financial allocation, lack of infrastructure, inadequate monitoring and poorly paid worker. Nearly 26 lakh workers, mostly women belonging to the backward sections of the society, who spend around 6 to 8 hr a day for the preparation, cooking and cleaning, are not recognized as workers. They are not paid anything near the mandated minimum wages, merely Rs 1000 per month, that too only for 10 months. After long year of services they are retrenched without any social security or pension, even though cases of accidents and burn are common, they are not covered under any insurance or medical benefits.

Sindhu, A (2014B) argued that the tragedy in Bihar, where 23 children,including two children of a mid day meal worker died after consuming the meal, brought into the national debate, the loopholes the scheme is suffering from. However, instead of taking necessary measure towards the effective implementation of the programe, the government was resorting to its privatization by handing it over to Corporate like Vedanta and to NGOs like Akshaya Patra Foundation, Naandi foundation etc. He further highlighted that these NGOs are supplying meals cooked in centralized kitchen located in places far off from the schools, going against the basis concept of providing freshly cooked hot meals of the children.Infact, to deliver on time, at what time they might have started preparing the food, packing, delivering to the school and how much time it took in distribution. These needs to be explore. We should not generalize if Akshaya Patra is doing well;rest of the agencies is also doing well. Henceforth we can't just promote PPP model just because one agency is performing well.

Press Trust India,(Dec 20,2013) PTA teachers field a PIL in the Court who said the free meal programme has increased their workload. Under the Government run scheme, added responsibility had been given to the teaching to supervise its implementation. It includes placing order for food, unloading food articles from vehicles in school premises, maintaining records of stock, disturbing meal and checking their quality before being served to pupils. under Section 27 of the Right to Education Act, non teaching work cannot be allotted to teachers and principals except that Census, elections and disaster relief.

PAISA (2012A) investigated the fund flow and food grain flows in Bihar and Utter Pradesh. They observed that the food grain flow management suffers from several inefficiencies. Records for monitoring food grain flows are poorly found. The district administration does not have a system to capture to actual lifting of food grains by the school. It was also found that there a huge gap in data of food grains allotted and actually lifted, as the state only lifted 51% of its annual allocation. When compared with school level food grain receipt data, they found evidences that these delays in lifting at the school level have repercussions on grain availability in schools. For Instead in Bihar, school level data pointed towards gaps between food grain stocks available in schools and food grains required for serving under MDM in accordance with the norms. It regards to fund flow, it was captured that was overall weak management at levels of transition, banking system, administration, limited staff. (Most officials interviewed argued that there not enough staff at their disposal to verify records collected from schools, issues section orders and monitor fund receipts at the school level). During field work, the PAISA team discovered that there are large information deficits at the school level regarding the timing and quantum of cooking costs that schools receive.

PAISA(2012B) observed in the district of Hardoi that there is lack of transparency in monitoring systems. No systems to weigh food grain as they were in route through delivery to schools. Food grains are packed at the FCI mills in bags each. These bags are never weighed after they leave the mills. In interviews, with block and school level officials it was discovered that it is common phenomena for schools in all districts to receive anywhere between 5 to 8 kgs less weight for every 50 kg bag of food grains. In the absence of adequate weighing facilities at the local godown, PDS shop and schools, it is difficult to pinpoint the specific link in the system at which the problem occurs. It was also found that there is a poor management for grain storage at ground level. Weak capacity was also a major issue in implementation. An oft-repeated issue that emerged at district level was the lack of adequate staff. In UP there is no dedicated staff for implementing and monitoring MDM at the block level. District officials argued that this was an important reason why they were unable to adequately track the flow of grains and meals at the school level. Thus they were unable to identify inefficiencies and bottlenecks in the process. In Bihar, interviews highlighted that the block level SFCs were understaffed, resulting in any delays for local contractors to lift food grains and deliver them to schools.

DARPG (2012) conducted a pilot study on Mid-day meal scheme in Dungarpur district, of Rajasthan, to identify key issues being faced by the implementation agencies and were able to validate the risks identified in the Risk classification framework. First they identified budgeting and forecasting as an associated risk from framework where the funding as per the norms was found to be inadequate. The 2nd associated risk from framework was identified as infrastructure, where drinking water facility was not available in most of the places. The transporters that have been entrusted with the responsibility of providing the grains to the schools were found avoiding travelling to the interiors of the districts. Thus, the demand is not covered by the transport supplies. It was also found that the system of monitoring is being defeated by the lack of infrastructural facilities available with the block level officers. It was reported that no local conveyances or facilities/allowance are provided to them for the purpose monitoring the implementation of MDMS effectively. Third was associated risk from framework to counter productivity in scheme where the cooks who were entitled to receive Rs 0.30 paise per child day, in case, where there are only 50 or less students, but the maximum wages received were only Rs 15 per day. Hence cooks were more interested to work in some other scheme (NREGS) where they get Rs 100 per day. Fourth associated risk from framework was implementing agency effectiveness where they found the gram panchayat who has been delegated with the responsibility of the implementation showed no or negligible interest in the process. In their place the teachers who were supposed to be in classroom for teaching were busy in providing the necessary facilities for the implementation of the scheme. Fifth associated risk from framework was community involvement; it was found that the micro-nutrients tablets were being provided to the children on a regular basis. Some tribal parents even opposed the giving of tablets. It was also observed that when the functioning of cooking was assigned to Naandi foundation, the schools reported cases of children not eating meals. The reason was meals cooked by Naandi don't match the local taste of the tribal children. Sixth associated risk from framework was health and safety/environment. It was found that there was no space for ventilation for smoke exit in the kitchen maintained by the schools. As it adversely impacted health of the cooks involved. In almost all the selected schools in Doongarpur district fire wood is used instead of LPG or smokeless chulhas. Reasons reported where there is shortage of LPG gas in the district. Seventh associated risk from framework was information, education and communication where it was found that parents involvement in MDMS was very less due to lack of awareness and benefits of the scheme. In village where parents are working under some scheme they usually asked their children to sit at home and do household works. Eighth associated risk from framework was capacity building, it was found that there was lack of availability of skilled data entry operators and dedicated management information system (MIS) cell at district level. Incomplete information was provided by the schools was also a major issue reported by the officers. This study indeed a very informative for internal stakeholders to rework the governance policy and find out the risk for its overall performance rather focusing only on enrollment. Attributes related to risk might vary according to geographical terrain. The limitation of this study is, they have not discussed how to handle such issues at different level of implementation and what are the other options to minimize this risk.

Rukmani. R(2011) The MS Swaminathan Research Foundation has prepared the documents on Indian experience with regard to feeding. The study found that the key problem in implementation was linked with both the quantum of funds and the flow of funds in the scheme. Until the revised norms of 2006 which came into effect, the States, on their part, pleaded serious financial constraints in mobilizing the resources for cooking costs. Subsequent experience has shown that even the revised norms did not solve the resources problem completely, even without ensuring legal minimum wages for cooks and helper, the cooking costs have gone up. The cost estimates for food grain and other ingredients consumed in the mid day meal also face upward pressure in view of the uncertain situation on the grain front and inflationary pressures in the economy. Even in 2006, the planning Commission working group noted that 'A large number of states continue to face financial difficulties in meeting cooking costs and providing cooked meals. It also recommended that the minimum cost norm for mid day meal should be raised from the present 'Rs 2 per child per day to Rs 3 per child per day. And this norm should be automatically adjusted for inflation every two years using the food component of the wholesale price index. There is a need to provision for training and skill up-gradation for staff in the scheme for information, education and communication, especially to disseminate messages of health and nutrition.

Sinha Dipa(2008A) about 55 lakh children are beneficiaries of the MDMS in 2006-07. To increase community monitoring of the MDMS, the government of Andra Pradesh initiated a social audit in five districts of the state. This social audit was conducted during the period January to April 2008 in 111 schools- 54 schools in Adilabad and 57 schools in Komool. The social audit team visited the schools unannounced during lunch time and did a physical verification of the number of children eating the mid day meal (head count) was further compared with the number that was recorded as having the meal in the attendance register. Author highlighted that while on the day of the social audit an average of 6755 children were found to be having meal, the attendance registers showed 8016 children as eating the meal. Further investigation found that there is an over-reporting of attendance. The reason behind doing such type of fraud is to get more funds as the fund received is insufficient for cooking. Henceforth social auditing by community plays an important role in making program successful but for this they should be involved and value the importance of social auditing.

Sinha,Dipa (2008B) revealed that, in Kumool district, village Bollagutta, on an average only 25-30 children came to school, but 70-80 children were marked present. Even the rice stock register showed that 9kg of rice was cooked, whereas the headmaster gave only 3-4 kg to the cook every day. When this was reported in the gram sabha, the headmaster confessed to committing fraud and immediately gave the sarpanch money for 50 kg of rice. The stock registers were only filled at the end of the month without checking the actual amount of rice cooked. Release order was not available in most schools. This shows policy gap and lack of monitoring and accountability of officials.

Performance Audit Report, Comptroller and auditor General, India (CAG) (2008) report on MDM, revealed that data from various states reveal that projected enrolment, on which food grain disbursement are made, were unrealistically high compared to historical and actual enrolment. This excess withdrawal of food grains creates scope for food grains to be diverted for unintended purposes. There have been several instances of mismatches in utilization of cooking costs and food grains procured by states. Not only that there have been mismatches between food grains supplies by the FCI and that procured by state agencies. None of the states were able to furnish utilization certificates nor had they identified ways to reduce theft and misuse. Moreover, 9 states did not monitor the quality of meals and the other states conducted irregular or no onsite inspections. Additionally, MoHRD did not provide micronutrient supplements, which it claimed was the states responsibility. CAG audit concluded that MoHRD had overlooked its crucial role in mission to ensure the provision of micronutrient supplements despite its focus on improving nutritional status of primary school children. Despite stated objectives to boost universalization of primary education, retention or attendance. Data collected from states on enrolment were being used solely for allocating food grains. Nor had MoHRD collected data on nutritional status of beneficiaries or established linkages with the ministry for family and health welfare to provide health check-ups as prescribed in the guideline. This report highlights lack of coordination between departments and lack of accountability among internal stakeholders.

2.4.1 REPORTED CASES OF ILL MANAGED MID-DAY MEAL SCHEME ACROSS COUNTRY

Besides several research/academic studies, there were large number of cases reported on MDM by local and national news paper. They were as follows:

Press Trust India, Jul 11,2014-in Bihar where 23 children died of poisoning in 2013. Where the lunch was provided under the government sponsored MDM scheme without checks or monitoring by local officials. Although it is the first such disaster in the project that feeds about 120 million children every day across India.

The poisoning, which police suspect was caused by storing cooking oil in a used pesticide container, killed the children so quickly that some died while being taken to hospital.

Press Trust India, Jul 14,2013- Two audit reports by the state governments of Andra Pradesh and Madhya Pradesh have said the food grains in the scheme was often laced with stones and worms.

Press Trust India, Jul 16, 2013- Survey done by the India Institute of management reported that children in Gujarat were made to wash up their plates after their meals by 'rubbing the soil on the plates and then giving a quick rise.'

Press Trust India, Jul 26, 2013-PATNA, Director Bihar MDM scheme R Lakhaman told PTI that MDM could not be served in over 4,600 schools affecting nearly 10 lakhs student for the second consecutive day in Bihar due to primary school teachers boycotting the duties,' As per the reports, MDM could not be served in over 4600 schools across the state out of a total of 70,000 schools covered by the program. About 10 lakhs students have been deprived of the meals due to boycott. The government agrees that basic job of the primary teachers is to teach and not supervise cooking of meals. But till some alternative arrangements are made they should cooperate in successful run of the scheme.

Press Trust India, Jul 27,2013, Orissa: An insect was found in the meal, supplied by a private agency, in a primary school at Hinjili in Odisha's Ganjam district. The meal was not served to any student when the insect was found on Friday in the Soya curry at Regedi Primary school Hinjli, Local Block Development Officer (BDO), Sunhransu Mishra said. The MDM was returned to Nandi Foundation immediately.

The below graph illustrated on the basis of literature reviewed that highlights inefficacy of policy, policy gap, weak monitoring, financial constrain, lack of coordination. In addition, it was found that most of the criticism was made against two levels regarding the effective implementation of MDMs i.e. central /state government and school at grass root level. If we see from the broader perspective, there are various stakeholders' involved in different stages of implementation. Henceforth, issues linked with the process of implementation are not always depends either top or bottom levels.

Figure 8: Steps of Governance of Mid-day meal, Issues related to implementation and governance

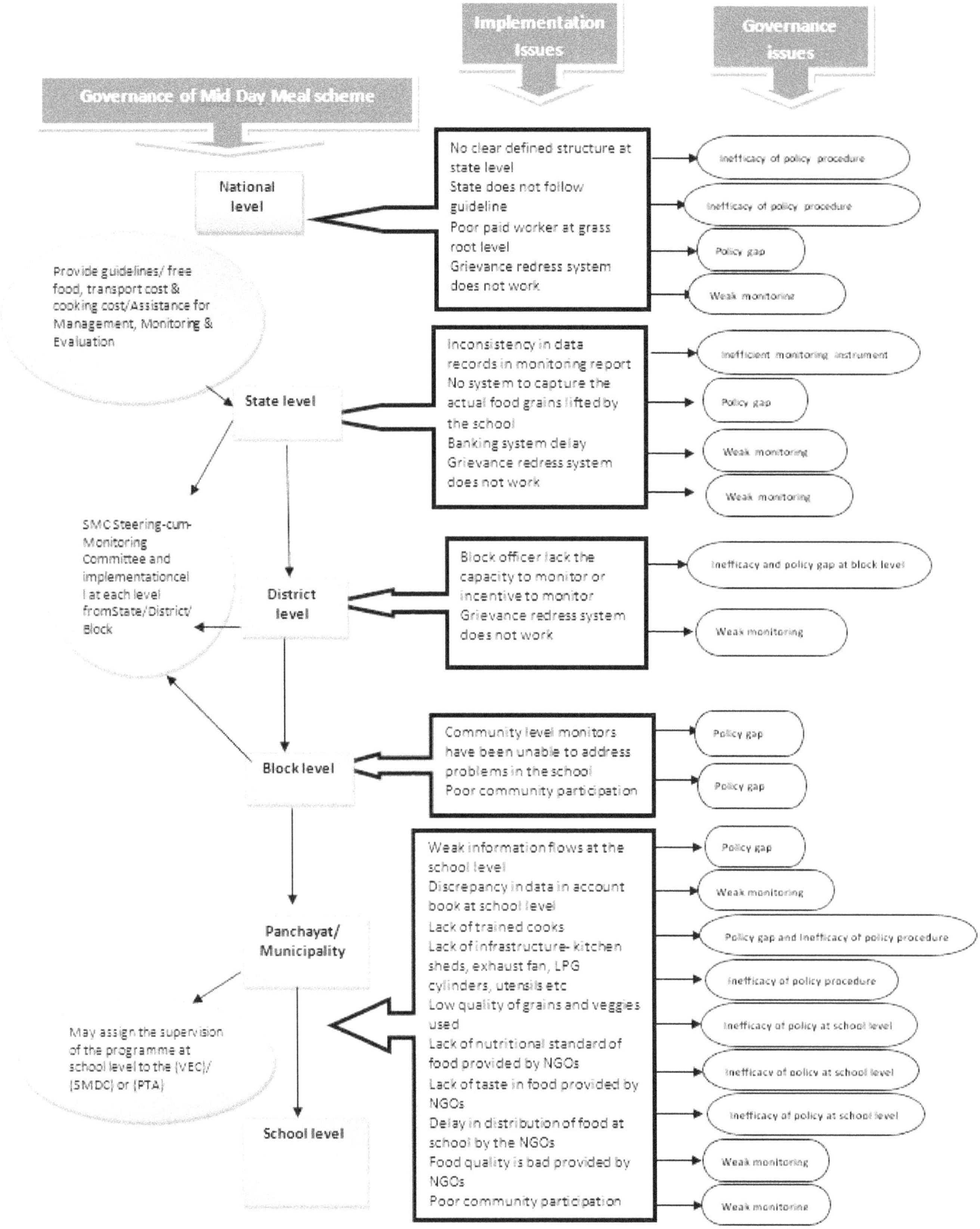

2.5 POLICY PLANNING AND PROCESS

Mathur, Kuldeep (2001), paper traced the evaluation of public policy process in India. The Author argued that the policy processes are constrained and influenced by the fact that India is still in a transition towards a more meaningful and participative democracy, despite having formal democratic institutions since Independence. This affects the policy process in two distinct ways. He explained that how on one hand, government tend to concentrate on their political survival rather than on policy and on the other hand, the bureaucracy still follows the colonial administration that is massive, self interested and not very effective. These political and bureaucratic characteristics have lent the Indian Policy-making process a decisively technocratic quality. Author further explained that there is a technical team appointed for policy formation. These committees handled specific policy issues or sectors and the members are required by political or civil servant elites who seek a quick policy proposal or recommendation. Very recent development is involvement of Research Institute. But the problem is they are challenged by resource constraints and have to toe a political line for more funding. All these factors have made independent analysis on policy issues a rare phenomenon. Author ads that it is only recently that non-government organization (NGOs) have started to challenge policy choices and have come up with alternatives. They influence policy processes in various ways, and offer the best possibility for alternative policy advice and choice. Author argued, however, NGOs role is limited by political and administrative constraints, the 'right to information' is crucial for more accountability and for expanding the possibility of alternative policy advice. I think in this type of situations, managerial studies need to be done. For example stakeholder mapping exercises where identifying internal and external stakeholders, their position, the level of power, their interest etc. as this will help to identify the area that need to work for better coordination and implementation of the policy.

Laurence J.O'Toole Jr.(2001), Author argues that while policy implementation no longer frames the core question of public management and public policy, some scholars have debated appropriate steps for revitalization. Because the practical world is in need a valid knowledge about policy implementation. Author questioned that where has all policy implementation gone? What has the field accomplished? Should a resurgence of attention to the subject be exhorted? And if it so, in what direction? This article considers these questions as main focus of as assessment of the state of the field, and the argument reaches somewhat unconventional conclusion. Authors suggested that an initial assessment is likely to understand the extent of work underway on matters quite close to the implementation theme. Authors suggested that policy and management are the relevance theme in policy implementation work. Research should be the base for any policy implementation. What are the resources available, how to use such resources, what would be the mechanism, how to involved stakeholders, how to divide their role and responsibility for achieving the goal. In general, without doing baseline studies, it is very tough to achieve the objectives by using best use of resources available.

Edward A.Morash and Daniel F.Lynch (2002), in their article, 'increasingly competitive and global markets', insisted that public policy should be customer focused in terms of stressing resources, capabilities and performance. This will help in ensure successful public/private partnerships, performance outcomes that are customer driven, planning and policy oversight that is performance based. The Author investigated the relative importance and availability of supply chain capabilities and performance for more than 3500 firms in three global regions: North America, Europe, and the Pacific Basin. The authors presented additional analysis for best practice firm that score the highest on an excellence index. The study found that public policy should be enabled customer service or demand oriented performance capabilities. Infact both are important. The study findings have important implication for international public policy, such as trade policies by linking policy priorities with private sector requirements for specific capabilities, resources and performance. Over all it is suggested that supply chain mechanism is needed for public policies implementation with supporting marketing capabilities of standardization, adaptation or customization of government planning, policy formulation and data availability.

Agarwal.O.P, Somnathan.T.V. (2005),this paper has focused why India's policy making structure have so much difficulty in formulating the 'right' policy and then sticking to it. It goes on to ask, the question of what can be done to improve the structures and systems involved in the making of public policy in India. According to him, public policy making in India has frequently been characterized by a failure to anticipate needs, impacts or reactions which could have reasonably been foreseen, thus impeding economic development.Author claims that policies have been reversed or change more frequently that warranted by exogenous changes or new information. Author argues that country like India with so much diversity, policy making process is a very complex task for policy makers. Author claims that history reveals that India due to either adopting wrong policies or poorly implementing the right public policies are the reason for under development or under performed country. Authors insisted that there can be valid disagreements/debates prior to the policy making on to what is the right policy in a given sector, in a given situation needed. The paper concentrates on quality of policy making within a broad sector rather than on issues of strategic choice between sectors. In this paper author discussed about the attributes of the policy making, what are the weakness in India's public policy making, why there is a need in reforming institutional structure and processes and finally the need of improving the competence and skill of policy making manpower in details. Author also proposed the steps that are required to be taken while preparing the public policies and try to avoid constraints while implementation.

Carolyn J.Hill, Laurance E. Lynn Jr. (2005), Author explains the focus of administrative practice is shifting from hierarchical government toward greater reliance on horizontal, hybridized and associational forms of governance. Author noted that the recent arguments to this effect, however, make limited recourse to the body of empirical evidence that might shed light on the actual extent of this transformation. In this article, author focus on the review of over 800 individual research studies in order to assess what they know about governance based on available empirical evidence across a range of disciplines and substantive fields. Author found that hierarchical investigations of the nature and consequences of governmental action predominate in the literature. Author supplemented this primary finding with additional analysis of research on performance and on public management.

PaudelN.R (2007), this paper critically examined the theory of public policy implementation of different generation, highlighted the issues on policy implementation studies and examined the applicability of such theory. This paper extensively reviewed the literature related to the public policy implementation, in first generation focused was more on uncertain relationship between policies, decision and implemented programs. Similarly, the second generation implementation studies focused on the development of an analytical framework in implementation, which included the top down, bottom up perspectives and their synthesis. Similarly, the third generation, author suggested that implementations research should concentrate on explicit implementation theory-building, which has not yet been realised. While reviewing the implementation literature, authors argued that the concrete theory of policy implementation literature is still lacking. Author claim that the literature surveyed in the article is dominated by the top down and bottom up perspectives and their synthesis. The basic arguments of these perspectives concern methodologies and accountability.

Smith B. Gail. (2008), this paper reviewed the opportunity available for food business to encourage consumers to eat healthier and more nutritious diets, to investigate in more sustainable forms of agriculture. The key factors in developing more sustainable supply chains are identified as the type of supply chain involved and the individual business attitude to extending responsibility for product quality into social and environmental performance within their own supply chains. Author insisted that interpersonal trust and working to standards are both important to build more sustained local and many conserved food supply chains. Author suggested that cooperation among food manufacturers, retailers, NGOs, government and farmer organizations is vital in order to raise standards for supply chains and to enable farmers to adopt more sustainable agriculture practices.

Benn Denis (2009), this article points out the inescapable nexus between ethics, social capital and governance. The aim of this paper is to examine the nature of this relationship and its implications for the formulation of public policy. Author argued that the concept of governance, which has been defined as the exercise of political, economic and administrative authority to manage a national affairs has undergone significant change in recent years. It is increasingly being interpreted to encompass the activities carried out by non-states actors, such as private sector, labour unions and other non government organisations. After detailed discussion author concluded that ethical consideration are an important aspect of public policy formulation and implementation in the overall governance process. Along with social capital that is equally important implication for the governance process since such group often exercises an important influence on the direction of public policy. In this paper author suggested types of governance and its implications in details.

S.Nambiyar,et,.al.(2010) in this article author highlighted involvement of Public Private Partnership in various sectors like infrastructure, education, health, housing and water etc. Author suggested that this model has also given a scope and direction to the corporate sector through their Corporate Social Responsibility program. Author added that it also gives an opportunity for major public sector companies to go beyond the scope of business relationship and improve their goodwill among stakeholders. Therefore author suggested that there should be a call for public private partnership (PPP) to achieve excellence in public service delivery in development sectors. Further highlighted that in Gujarat the MDM has been strengthened with the interventions of private and corporate partnerships and highlighted that this is an example of innovations in delivery of public services through Private partner. The study found that the filed study reinforces the widely held belief that participation of private sectors brings improvement to public services in term of investments, efficiency, accountability and effective services delivery. Author claims that such model not only empowers the citizens but also enables the governments in facilitating quality service delivery. Moreover when quality services are delivered within a transparent framework people are able to exercise their choice in availing services.

J.Mc Manus,(2008) the author define the meaning of governance perspective all about. He believes that many organisations run on the basis of Ideology (beliefs). As the beliefs differ, conflict exists between power seeker and stakeholders. The author belief that for the governance perspective, all organisations are social institutions with hierarchy and power. Where business is manage by owner and manager who in theory are responsible for their own action of their subordinates. After analyzing evolution of governance author concluded that regardless the responsibilities carried out by the broad depend mainly on different legal regulations, dispersion of ownership, director's attitude, director's willingness to take responsibility, attention to duty, ability to assess the firm environment, organisation, personal and private affairs, as well as resulting financial accounting practices and remuneration. He further suggested that efficiency of the governance get lower than expected due to the deficiencies in some or all stated factors. The author finally recommended the important factors that influence the outcome of governance is more focus on ethics, legal framework, code of guidelines by linking primarily to the level of knowledge and skill and not so much their power in an organisation.

World Bank (2012) report on Safety Net MDM India, in their inspection report it was highlighted that in India, procuring rice directly from the farmers is not feasible because the food for the MDM is mandated to be channeled through the public distribution system. However, the decentralization nature of the programe allows for some differentiation on programme design and procurement practices. Implementation design of Kerala is discussed as there procurement arrangement involve local farmers selling paddy directly to mill owners, who in turn sell rice to authorized wholesalers who then distribute it to fair-price shops. Unfortunately, progamme flaws seriously limited the local procurement aspects. Reasons mentioned was lack of smooth flow of funds, resulting in difficulties in maintaining steady procurement commitments which are necessary for local small scale farmers, risk for the municipality that local agriculture initiatives might not be able to supply required amount of produce at all times. Risk for farmers that they might not be able to honor contract commitments at all times finally it is difficult in adjusting supply and demands during vacation time and unexpected school holidays.

2.6 SUPPLY CHAIN MECHANISM

Lu.Dawel (2011) wrote a book 'fundamental of supply chain management' define, 'Supply chain is mainly a group of different actions that any organisation adopts for better delivery and produce useful product or services. This term was used in 1985 by 'Michal Porter'. He provided a structure through how to generate benefits and find out the loopholes in the process as well as where we can add value addition or delete some activities that can enhance the process. At the most fundamental level, supply chain management (SCM) is management of the flow of good, data, and finances related to a product or services, from the procurement of raw materials to the delivery of the product at its final destination. Although many people equate supply chain with logistic. Logistics is actually just one component of the supply chain. Today's digital based SCM systems include material handling and software for all parties involved in product or service creation, order fulfillment and information tracking such as suppliers, manufactures, wholesalers, transportation and logistics provider, and retailers. And when it comes to supply chain sustainability, responsible organisation act by creating a governance structure. Governance structure ensure that company decisions align with stated company value and can provide the data and transparency that is increasingly in demand. Governance takes a more holistic view of the system and synergies between the players. A weak or non –existent supply chain governance strategy leads to poor transparency and weakens the foundation of your supply chain. Basically governance ensures you have the correct resources and capabilities there when u need them. It is important to note the difference between supply chain management and supply chain governance: supply chain management is concern with the operation side and strategic coordination of partner actions, whereas, supply chain governance integrates coordination of operations and ensures that proper policies are implemented and controlled. It means taking intentional actions to affect partner relationships. Supply chain governance creates leverage and scale; help manage risk, increases bottom line profitability and comfort to your regulatory, social and environment friendly company agenda. It is multidimensional and includes initiating, developing and maintaining relationships between each 'link' in supply chain. It coordinates the way financial, material and human resources are earmarked within the flow and the framework for decision making'.

Mechanism for governance can include contracts, standards, mechanisms for reporting, and social bond. Key components include: Working collaboratively to plan, establish and communicate overall policy guidelines, minimum expectations of performance, assessed risk, and mitigation plan and compliance metrics.Providing visibility into supply chain Expenditures Company –wide through functional categories and contract compliance. Planning and executing essential initiatives while incorporating supply chain governance attributes. Tracking, auditing and reporting initiative status as well as key measures of governance across internal customer-facing department and external suppliers, carriers and intermediaries as well as stakeholders

Li Pengzhong (2011), defines supply chain management as the set of activities undertaken by an organisation to promote effective management of its supply chain. His paper investigated the possibility to merge lean, agile, resilient and green paradigms in the supply chain management. Further elaborate about paradigms have the same global purpose: to satisfy the customer needs, at the lowest possible cost to all members in the supply chain. It represent the first effort to 'drill down' the key attributes related the lean, agile, resilience and green paradigms development in a supply chain context, providing link between supply chain attributes, paradigms and supply chain performance. Therefore this chapter scientific contribution is twofold: first, contributes for research on supply chain management by providing links between the deployment of LARG_ SCM paradigms and supply chain performances; and second, it identifies synergies and divergences between the paradigms. For the managerial point of view it gives to supply chain manager's insights on how the adoption of paradigms will affect their network and how it can increase supply chain performance.

Kadari,R. and Roy,S.M. (2016) in their article 'Strengthening the MDMS through MIS and Interactive Voice Response System (IVRS) in Utter Pradesh',discussed the implementation of MDMP in India and the current system that is being used for implementation of the program. Author highlighted the current reporting structure of present model involved in the scheme, their drawbacks such as: under the scheme, records are to be maintained regularly and monthly reporting is to done without fail. A MDM register at school/block/district level for monthly physical and financial information is to be maintained which help is verification of facts. The school fills up the number of students availing MDM on daily basis in the school level in the MDM register. This helps in estimating the ration to be used each day and prevent wastage of food. This data provided by school is supposed to be compiled at the block level and further at the district level. After all compilation a Quality Progress Report (QPR) is generated through the system. The authors highlighted the use of MIS and Interactive Voice Response System (IVRS) are discussed in details and also suggested the road ahead so that better results can be reaped out of this program.

Srinivasan (2012) in his article 'Supply Chain Reform in Dairy Sector- India', discussed about the base of formation of Gujarat Cooperative Milk Marketing federation. He reported that to avoid middleman from the process the dairy farmer organized a huge strike in 1940's. They were totally against of middleman in this extended process, as they were exploited. Therefore value chain techniques were used to analyses the process and eliminate unwanted practice by Dr.Verghese Kurien .He established a direct linkage between milk producers and consumers.

Singh, Priyanka,.etal.,(2018) submitted dissertation on network Design in Mid Day Meal program in Utter Pradesh, reported that currently centralized kitchen (Akshya Patra's Foundation) is facing the challenge of fulfilling the growing demand of meals within short delivery window while keeping the transportation cost and the fixed costs of the kitchens low. Keeping in mind that food is a highly perishable item and has a very short delivery window (four hours), they designed a kitchen network to solve Akshaya Patra's Foundation problem by using an optimization method called Mixed Integer Liner Programming (MILP). They also tested various scenarios such as network design considering kitchen's capacity constraint; design with cross docking, and the use of insulated constrainers. Their model suggests a network design approach using cross docking and insulated containers. The proposed model has lowest cost and can be replicated in other state also.

Sabkota,Ranjita (2015) submitted report on Value Chain Analysis of MDMS in Karnataka. She conducted the study in five district of the selected state based on qualitative data collection. She highlighted that till date whatever implementation issued happened only centre or school level were blamed. She elaborated the implementation process through Map using the basic concepts of value chain analysis technique.

Roy, Vivek., et al.(2017) conducted the study 'Supplier participation towards addressing sustainability-oriented objectives of the mid day meal supply chain: Insights from The Akshya Patra Foundation, India' with the purpose to explore and further explain the phenomena of supplier participation in addressing the sustainability –oriented objectives of a supply chain. Specifically the paper explains how a buyer can integrate sustainability concerns among its suppliers. The study is based in the context of the Indian school feeding (Mid Day Meal) program and approach the issue from the perspective of a mid day meal provider. Authors first explained how the mid day meal providers in India explicitly address the social and economic dimensions of sustainability. Thereby, conducts an exploratory case study on a renowned meal provider with the objective to understand the nature of its efforts towards supplier participation through indepth interviews. An evident in the case, from the buyer's perspective, the key to success in winning supplier participation for addressing sustainability oriented supply chain objectives largely revolves around three critical aspects. First, it is essential to develop a detailed purchasing and supply policy for addressing the sustainability requirements of the supply chain. Second, apart from the development of policy, the implementation of the policy needs to be surrounded with the complex efforts for generating a compliance and commitment among suppliers. Third, the needed compliance and commitment toward the policy largely depends on the efforts in building favorable intent among suppliers- towards addressing the sustainability concern of the supply chain. The present paper therefore outlines the central importance of the notion of efforts and challenges in understanding suppliers' participation in a SSCM environment. Generating insights into these aspects, the present research emphasized critical implications surrounding SSCM theory and practices. The study highlighted a range of context –specific best practices around the identified critical aspects. As far as limitations are concerned.

World Bank group (2015), report on Education global practices, in 2015 with the partnership of World Food Program, they developed the toolkit SABER (System Approach for the Better Education Result) for reviewing different health and education policies globally. It's an initiative to produce comparative data and knowledge based on supply chain mechanism on education policies and institution, with the aim of helping countries systematically strength their education systems and the ultimate goal of promoting learning for All. It allows country to conduct a thorough inventory of their education policies and institutions based on global best practices as well as provide decision maker and stakeholders to take best decision for betterment. Based on extensive research on supply chain mechanism and global evidences the tool is based on LeanPrincipals and focused on five core areas for better implementation. The core dimension is like national policy framework, institution capacity and coordination, sound design and implementation and community roles.

2.7 THEORITICAL FRAMEWORK

LEAN PRINCIPLES

Lean is a concept, a philosophy, a practice and a set of tools all wrapped in one. For more than 50 years, organizations have been invested time and money adopting the principles of lean (while originated at Toyota Corporation for manufacturing operations, the principles of lean have since spread to many types of businesses and functional areas). The focus of lean is to maximize quality, minimize unnecessary steps and optimize costumer value (provide them what they want when they want it). A lean organization focuses on providing the best quality within the shortest possible lead time, while minimizing waste throughout the processes (waste being classified as any resource that is not being used properly). We may first think that minimizing waste means minimizing inventory, time, effort and people are also resources to be utilized properly. Analyzing how people are used and time is spent is a critical step in minimizing waste. By adopting lean principles in supply chain planning can help in achieving the biggest objectives which are to reduce cost and improve customer services.

A series of conceptual tools which have evolved from 'Toyota Production System' can be applied to Supply Chain Planning in any organization. They are as follows: 1)**Just in Time (JIT)** ensures all efforts are directed at providing only the goods and services required by the customers, both, when they want it and in the exact quantity they desire. The goals of JIT are aligned with the goals of supply chain planning.2) **Value Stream Mapping** involves mapping out all the steps of your processes, including the flow, timing of each step and waited times for all associate activities. Value Stream mapping identifies and eliminates waste. There is no doubt that mapping out the various processes in Supply Chain Planning and how they are all connected will lead to better understanding of the value of each step and how to streamline and eliminate non-value added activities.

Henceforth, in the current study the researcher adapted the tools developed byWorld Bank World Food program as a base for further analysis. The tool is developed with the lens of Lean Principals of Supply Chain

Mechanism. As it provided the comprehensive assessment of the governance of the program that has the following in place: (1) National Policy Framework (2) Sufficient institutional capacity and coordination (3) Stable funding (4) Sound design and implementation (5) Community participation. With the help of above frameworks the study describesthe governance of program by the key supply chain relationships including policy guidelines, flow of grains, fund and information between actors across system, examining the advantages and disadvantages of different design options (centralized and decentralized kitchen), Risk factors and internal / external factors that effecting the process.

Figure 9: Internal and external factors influencing the process

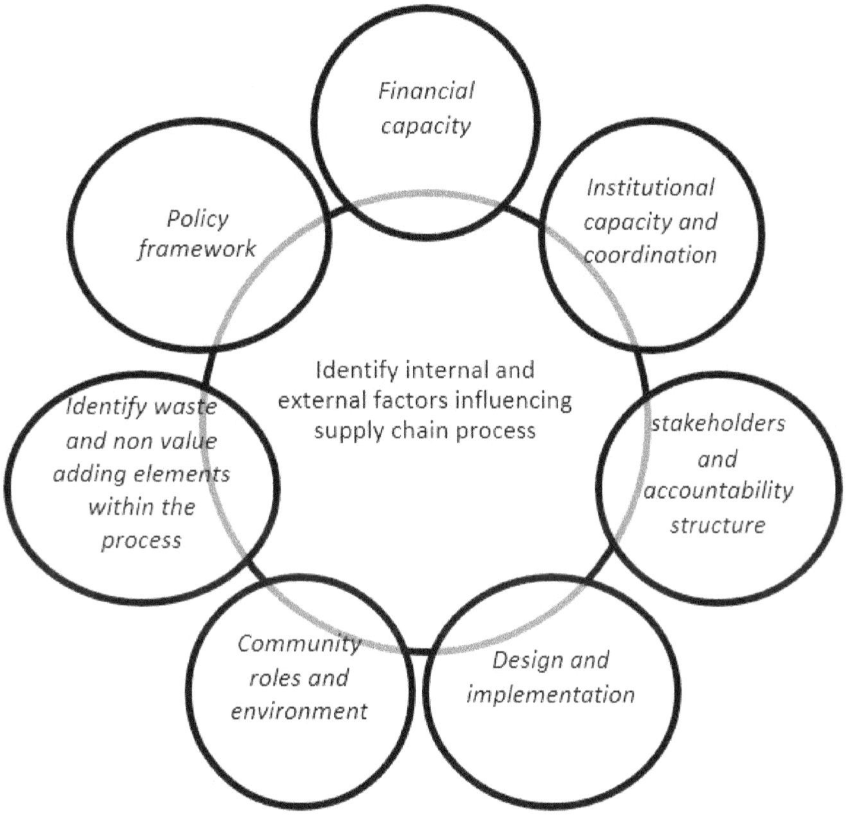

*Henceforth ,*supply chain technique under lean principles and tools developed is used to identify the systematic approach in process improvement involving the following steps in this research:

CHAPTER III

METHODOLOGY

This chapter describes the process and research method adopted for data collection with the support of conceptual framework of supply chain.

3.1 CONCEPTUAL FRAMEWORK

At National level in 1995 Nutritional Support to Primary Education was launched. In 2001, the Indian Supreme Court passed a landmark decision on right to food, mandating that all public schools should provide cooked meals. MDMS is a centralized scheme and in all government and government aided schools hot meals are been served to the children. The main objectives of the programme were to increase enrollment, retention and improve child nutrition.

Within this long gap of more than 20 years of governance, there is a list of reviews that suggested that the Flagship programme has been hampered from different dimensions. Deviation from standard norms in financial allocation, flow of food grains, funds and information, process of implementation, monitoring mechanism and quality of food provided to the beneficiaries were frequently reported. Therefore, it is an appropriate stage to assess the efficiency of governance framework through supply chain analysis techniques as we all know that MDMS is a complex form of intervention. According to Kretschmer et al. (2012), supply chain management is a key factor for program delivery and performance of its complex form of intervention. Recent years many organisations whether it is Business /Non Business, are now accustom with this mechanism for better output. So the question is 'why now?' A convincing answer to this question is that our business environment has changed, which includes globalisation, more severe competition, heighten customer expectation, technological impact and geopolitical factors and so on. Under such a renewed business environment, an organisation focused management approach is no longer adequate to deliver the required competiveness. Stakeholders must therefore understand that their business is only part of the supply chains they participated and it is the supply chain that wins or loses the competition. Thus the arena of competition is moving from 'organisation against organisation' to 'supply chain against supply chain'. The survival of a business today is no longer solely dependent on its own ability to compete but rather on the ability to cooperate within the supply chain. The seemingly independent relation between the organisations within the supply chain becomes ever more interdependent. You 'sink or swim with the supply chain.' This is the reason that gives rise to the need for the supply chain management (Lu. Dawel, 2011).

As we already discussed that Mid Day Meal Scheme is a complex intervention (multistage, multi sector, multiple activities starting from production, procurement, trading, preparation consumption, involvement of different actors (supplier, transporter, government, third party) that took place at different levels. It is therefore recommended to study MDMS governance from supply chain perspective. For the current study, after studying multiple techniques, the researcher further adopted multiple set of tools wrapped in one technique that is lean principles for further analysis. With the help of this framework the study describes the governance of program by the key supply chain relationships including policy guidelines, flow of grains, fund and information between actors across system, examining the advantages and disadvantages of different design options (centralized and decentralized kitchen). Henceforth supply chain technique under lean principles and tools is used to identify the systematic approach in the implementation of the policy at grass root level by linking the following in the study-

- To find out internal and external factors influencing supply chain process in terms of policy framework, financial capacity, institutional capacity and coordination, management and accountability structure, design and implementation, community roles and school environment

- To find unwanted activities that is just wasting of time/money/manpower/ resources

Accordingly, the study identified the internal and external factors affecting the governance of Mid Day Meal Scheme with respect to beneficiaries, suppliers, third parties, resource providers and internal factors including supply chain strategy (with the elements, priorities, targeting and hot cooked meal and centralized and decentralized mechanism)also tried to identify and eliminate wastes (time, effort and material) during supply chain analysis.

In addition, digital application is being proposed for better connectivity and transparency in the implementation process. This application will be accessed by all the stakeholders (internal and external). They can receive information on quality/quantity and status of flows of fund/grains/other information on time. They can monitor supply chain activities. This approach will be helpful to all the stakeholders to take corrective measures. It is assumed that where (any states) MDM policy and governance is rooted through theoretical framework the probability of achieving the objectives is high and vice-versa. The study helped us in identifying the areas where restructuring is needed or there is a requirement of developing new areas for further intervention. Henceforth the theory of Supply Chain provides Roadmap, where an organization's governance structure can be reviewed in an organized and systematic manner in order to assure alignment of the supply chain with the programme objectives.

3.2 RESEARCH QUESTIONS:

1. To what extent there are similarities and gaps with the supply chain framework?

2. What are the areas where there are similarities and achieving the objectives?

3. What are the areas where there are gaps and not achieving the objectives?

3.3 MAIN OBJECTIVES:

- To study the extent of variance of governance in MDM programme from the supply chain framework

- To identify the areas where there is a need for reforms in the governance framework

3.4.1 RESEARCH DESIGN

The study is descriptive in nature and focused on governance of the scheme. Qualitative research methods are employed for data collection. Both primary and secondary sources were used for collecting data. The study adopted Lean principals of supply chain mechanism for constructing a base for comparing the governance framework. Researcher used the same indicators mentioned in the frameworks for preparing tools and in-depth analysis.

3.4.2. LIST OF INDICATORS AND THE RELATED INFORMATION ASSES

MDM policy instrument Indicators	Related information assessed
Policy Framework	Is MDM included in any published sectorial policy, strategy or law (e.g. education sector plan, nutrition strategy, social protection etc. What are the objectives?
Policy Framework	On what background MDMS formed? Is this evidence based policy?
Policy Framework	Is there a published national policy on MDM? Which sectors were involved in developing the policy? What are the guidelines of the policy?
Financial Capacity	Is MDM included in the national planning process and funded through a national budget? What is the approximate government's budget for MDM
Financial Capacity	What is the allocated budget for the national MDM programme per child/per year? How do they project? Explain
Financial Capacity	Does each ministry involved in the program have a budget line for MDM
Financial Capacity	Is the budget at the regional/district level for MDM enough to cover all the expenses for running the national programme in line with national policies and norms? Define
Financial Capacity	Do regions/districts have budget plans for MDM? What is the mechanism of developing budget plan? Explain
Financial Capacity	Is the budget at the school level for MDM enough to cover all the expenses for running the national programme in line with national policies and norms?
Financial Capacity	Do schools have budget plans for MDM? What is the process of preparing budget plan?
Institutional capacity and coordination	Is there a steering committee coordinating the implementation of MDM?
Institutional capacity and coordination	How often does this body meet? Does it have a clear work plan and objectives?
Institutional capacity and coordination	Who all are parts of this steering committee (e.g. Education, Health, Agriculture, Social Protection, Local Government, Water, etc.)
Institutional capacity and coordination	Are non-government partners involved in the steering committee meetings?
Institutional capacity and coordination	Is MDM discussed in any national-level coordination body (technical working group, task force, or the like) that deals with education, school health and nutrition, agriculture, food security, nutrition, or other
Management and the accountability structure	Is there a specific unit at the national level in charge of the overall management of MDM within the lead institution and responsible for coordination between the national, regional/local (if applicable) and school levels?
Management and the accountability structure/ stakeholders mapping	Does the responsible unit in charge of implementing MDM have a sufficient amount of staff given the responsibilities that the unit has been given?
Management and the accountability structure/ stakeholders mapping	How many stakeholders work in the national unit responsible for MDM? How many of them are internal stakeholders who all are fully dedicated to MDM (if any)?
Management and the accountability structure/ stakeholders mapping	Does the unit have stakeholders that are fully trained and knowledgeable on MDM issues?

MDM policy instrument Indicators	Related information assessed
Management and the accountability structure/ stakeholders mapping	Are there coordination mechanisms in place between government (national/regional/ school level) stakeholders? Please give a brief description of how these coordination mechanisms function
Management and the accountability structure/ stakeholders mapping	Is there any pre/in-service training program in place to train internal stakeholders at the national level on MDM?
Management and the accountability structure/ stakeholders mapping	Do regional/district offices have sufficient staff, knowledge and resources to fulfill their responsibilities?
Management and the accountability structure/ stakeholders mapping	Do schools have a mechanism to manage MDM, based on national guidance (such as national implementation guidelines or a manual)
Management and the accountability structure/ stakeholders mapping	Is there any pre/in-service training program in place to train relevant staff at local/school level on MDM program management and implementation?
Management and the accountability structure/ stakeholders mapping	Is there any role and responsibility for external stakeholders? How do you involve them and at what level?
Design and Implementation/ activities involved	How many students benefit from the national MDM programme? Please provide this information for the past three years
Design and Implementation/ activities involved	Is there a specific program implementation document for the national programme (e.g.operational guidelines or standards, implementation manual, implementation strategy…)?
Design and Implementation/ activities involved	Is there a government monitoring and evaluation plan or strategy for MDM at national and state level?
Design and Implementation/ activities involved	What are the mechanism used for monitoring and evaluation?
Design and Implementation/ activities involved	Is this M&E system integrated into a national monitoring or education management information system (EMIS)?
Design and Implementation/ activities involved	Are data collected and progress reports on MDM produced by the government at national level?
Design and Implementation/ activities involved	Are data collected and progress reports on MDM produced at regional level?
Design and Implementation/ activities involved	Are data collected and progress reports on MDM produced at school level?
Design and Implementation/ activities involved	Is the M&E data used to refine and update programs or components of programs? If yes, kindly Indicate which programme components have been reviewed based on M&E data
Design and Implementation/ activities involved	Have there been any base line and impact evaluations carried out, or are any planned?
Design and Implementation/ activities involved	Has the program's actual cost per child per year been calculated?
Design and Implementation/ activities involved	What are the national standard of food modality ?

MDM policy instrument Indicators	Related information assessed
Design and Implementation/ activities involved	Are these standards generally known and implemented at school level?
Design and Implementation/ activities involved	Is the M&E information used to refine and update food modalities on a periodic basis?
Design and Implementation/ activities involved	Are the national standards based on procuring as locally as possible? if yes, Do the national standards take into account the costs?
Design and Implementation/ activities involved	Do the national standards take into account the risks and challenges during implementation? How they are preparing for such circumstances?
Design and Implementation/ activities involved	Do the national standards take into account the production capacity in the country and include measures to ensure the stability of food supply?
Design and Implementation/ activities involved	Is an analysis of food requirements and supply options for MDM programmes done regularly?
Design and Implementation/ activities involved	Are there food quality norms and food quality control mechanisms?
Design and Implementation/ activities involved	Are the norms governing the procurement process available to the public (transparent) and implemented?
Design and Implementation/ activities involved	Have there been discussions on possible procurement modalities for MDM that can be more locally appropriate, including the possibility of linking procurement with agriculture-related activities (that is, local-level support to small-scale farmers)?
Design and Implementation/ activities involved	Are there service provision models that could potentially create jobs and profit-making opportunities for community members (e.g. in processing, cooking, etc.)?
Design and Implementation/ activities involved	Are there complementary programmes with budgets that provide capacity building of the community for the following-Storage, Food processing, Preparation, marketing?
Community Roles	Are there school committees that involves parents, teachers, and local community in the implementation of MDMs ? Explain
Community Roles	Are/were these committees involved in the design of the program?
Community Roles	Do the committees manage and monitor the MDM program and ensure appropriate utilization of the food in the school? Explain
Community Roles	Are the roles and responsibilities of the community clearly defined (e.g. in the national MDM policy or other policy document/guideline)?Define
Community Roles	How do communities work with the MDM programs?
Community Roles	What are the main constraints facing community involvement?
Psycho-Social School Environment	Are there any systematic mechanisms in place to respond to issues of stigmatization in schools across country? Explain
Psycho-Social School Environment	What are the mechanisms that are in place to systematically address issues of stigmatization in school? Eg- life skill education in curriculum, Pri service/inservice training etc
Psycho-Social School Environment	Are there support groups in place at the school level or community level to respond to specific stigma issues faced by teachers/cook and students? Explain
Psycho-Social School Environment	Does the national school curriculum cover any health, hygiene, and nutrition and life skill? Explain

MDM policy instrument Indicators	Related information assessed
Psycho-Social School Environment	if yes, are all schools teaching this curriculum?
Psycho-Social School Environment	Is there pre- and in-service training provided to teachers to teach this curriculum?
Psycho-Social School Environment	Is the health-related knowledge covered in this curriculum integrated into school examinations?

3.4.3 SUPPLY CHAIN CONFIGURATION

Key Activities Linking Food Production to Mid Day Meal Scheme

The supply chain description highlights the key activities linking from food production to consumption by beneficiaries. It shows the supply chain relationships between all the actors involved, e.g. flow of goods, funds and information. The supply chain description is structured along three dimensions, i.e., key activities in the supply chain, level of activity and actors involved in supply chain.

Table 2: Supply chain, level of activity and actors involved

Primary supply chain activities					
	Production	Trade	Procurement activities	Preparation activities	Consumption
	Actors involved				
Level of activities					
National level	Supplier	Supplier			
Regional level/ district level	Supplier	Supplier	Government		
School level				Third party	Beneficiaries

As mentioned above these are the key activities (production, trade, procurement, preparation and consumption) involved at different levels from national to school.

3.4.4 LIST OF VARIABLESAND THEIR OPERATIONAL DEFINATION ARE AS FOLLOWS-

VARIABLES	GENERIC/ OPERATIONAL DEFINATIONS
Community Roles	Special title been given to the community members who all are assign important work in planning and execution in MDMS.
Consumption	Refers to the end point in the supply chain process For this study the consumption refer the food provided to the children at school.
Financial Capacity	The financial limit of an organisations ability to absorb losses with its own funds or borrowed funds without major disruption.(Guidelines for Public Debt management-World Bank 2001) For this study, how much budget being sectioned/ allocation/department wise allocation, district/ block and school, how this fund being used/it is sufficient to fulfil the objective of the scheme or not?

VARIABLES	GENERIC/ OPERATIONAL DEFINATIONS
Flow of goods or transportation	Movement of goods at next activity level covering all stages (international, national, community etc.). For MDM, movement of grain from FCI to school, involvement of transporter and other stakeholders, duration, storage, quality, quantity, monitoring
Governance perspectives	Refer to "the process and structure used to direct and manage an organisations operation activity. Focus more on the utilization of resources effectively and ensure they are managed in the best interests of their principal stakeholders" Mc Manus.J,(2008). MDMS is a complex multilevel intervention. It's more like organisation. Different activities took place at different point of time. List of internal and external stakeholders involved in the process with their power and interest. Various departments involved in the implementation of the scheme. So it's time to focus and rethink about the process and by using the available resources effectively and efficiently.
Identifying value	"This is the first step in Lean management, means finding the problem that the customer needs solved and making the product the solution. Specifically, the product must be the part of the solution that the customers readily pay for. Any process or activity that does not add value- means it does not add usefulness, importance or worth- to the final product is considered waste and should be eliminated". (James p.womack, Danial T.Jones and Danial Roos 1991) Activities (that took place during flow of funds/information/grain and other materialetc) are time consuming, not cost effective, over burden, multiple channels for information, etc need to be identify that is not giving any value addition to the scheme is a waste.
Information flow	Refers to the exchange of information between supply chain actors. In MDM, flow of information related to grain, food items, oils, gas, enrolment, monitoring from both way top to bottom and visa versa.
Institutional capacity & coordination	'The United Nation Development programme (UNDP) and United Nation Disaster Risk Reduction Offices (UNISDR) in (2016) define institutional capacity as the capacity of an institution to set and achieve social and economic goal, through knowledge, skill, systems, resources (human, technical and financial) and institutions'. Regarding MDMS it refers, Is there a steering committee coordinating from national level, do they have work plan, how often they discuss the issues, through what channel, who all are involved etc
Lean management	'Is an approach to managing an organisation that supports the concept of continuous improvement, a long term approach to work that systematically seeks to achieve small, incremental changes in processes in order to improve efficiency and quality'.(womackJames p.,et.al.(1991) By using this approach the main purpose is to identify internal and external factors that are affecting the chain.
Management and the accountability structure	"An accountability structure is the organizational framework that depicts the different groups within the partnership and includes an outline of the roles and responsibilities of each group, describing the processes, people, and supports necessary to function effectively".(Accountability structure toolkit 2015). Regarding MDMS it refers, any specific unit at the national level in charge of the overall management of MDM for coordination between the national, regional/local (if applicable) and school levels, no of dedicated staff, their knowledge and skill, training, documentation etc.

VARIABLES	GENERIC/ OPERATIONAL DEFINATIONS
Money flow	Refers to the financial transactions in school feeding supply chains.
Operation activities	"All the activities that has been taken place within the organisation starting from making products to the end beneficiary".(HandsfieldRobert,B. (1999). Activities that take place from national to school level starting from policy formation, procurement, transportation, preparation and consumption comes under operational activities.
Organisation	"An organisation can be conceptualised as a collection of individuals deliberately structured within specific boundaries to achieve predetermined goals" (Robert,B. Handsfield(1999). MDMS consider as a big organisation with structured mechanism where internal and external stakeholders work together to fulfil the goal of the scheme.
Organisational goal	"Organisational goals are desired states of affaires or preferred results that organisations attempt to realise and achieve". (Handsfield,Robert,B. (1999). The main objective of the MDMS is to increase enrolment reduce dropouts, and improve health status by providing good quality and quantity of hot nutritious meal on time across country by using best use of resources available.
Organisational Resources	"Organisational resources are all assets that are available to a firm for use during the production process. The four basic types of organisational resources are human, monetary, raw materials and capital. Organisational resources are combined, used, and transformed into finished products during the production processes. (Handsfield.Robert,B. (1999)
Oversight and quality control that	Involve the monitoring and evaluation of programme activities, including inputs, process, outputs and outcomes (procurement, transportation, preparation and consumption)
Preparation and distribution	Involves the range of different activities generally undertaken at the school level.
Processing	Refers to value-adding processes such as packaging, milling, fumigation and pasteurisation. An additional special process may be fortification with micronutrients.
Procurement activities	Refer to food /grain and other food items, sourcing, buying and receipt of products.
Production	Refers to agricultural activities that include obtaining inputs, planting and maintaining, harvesting and final selling of products.
Psycho-Social School Environment	According to Haaetel and Walbeg (2007), psychosocial environment is a type of environment that has to do with interaction in the classroom. This interaction involves teacher and student, student and student, teacher, student and instructional material interaction. School should be child friendly. Where children should feel secured, have their identity, freedom of expression, learn, eat and play without any ill feeling. Henceforth, it is important to explore whether thereis any stigma related gender/class, among teacher/cook/ parents in school? If yes, Is there any coping mechanism to handle such situation.
Public policy	"Common way of understanding and engaging in public policy is through a series of stages known as "the policy cycle". The characterization of particular stages can vary, but a basic sequence is agenda setting- formulation-legitimating-implementation –evaluation". Haddad &Demsky (1995) MDMS was made in response to fulfill the gap and improve the education attainment of children by providing free hot nutritious meal at school premise. Comes under Law Right to Education (RTE) and Right to Food (RTF) with prescribed guidelines that need to be followed from top to bottom to achieve the goal.

VARIABLES	GENERIC/ OPERATIONAL DEFINATIONS
Resources	Include cash or in-kind supporting the program implementation and management.
Stakeholder	"Stakeholders refer to the manpower involved in the project/ program at different level of execution with their interest and potential".Gisclard, Henri. (2012)
Stakeholder mapping	"Process of drawing a visual representation of the various people involved in or affected by the project. This visual tool should provide a clear picture of who the various stakeholders groups are, as well as their motives and interest". Gisclard, Henri. (2012)
Supply chain management	"Defined as the design, planning, execution, and control and monitoring of supply chain activities with the objective of creating net value, building a competitive infrastructure, leveraging worldwide logistics, synchronising supply with demand and measuring performance globally". David Jacoby (2009)
Trade	Refers to a market intermediation function between product supply and product demand.
Vulnerabilities	Refer to key potential problem areas in a specific supply chain. They may arise in each stage of the supply chain and will have an impact upon supply chain performance (natural disaster, environmental risk, market related risk, logical infrastructure risk, managerial and operational risk, Political and security risk etc.
Warehousing	Refers to storage of food products over time.

3.4.5 STUDY AREA -TAMIL NADU &GUJARAT

Both the states initiated this programe before independence.The programme has been implemented differently in both the states.In current scenario wherein Gujarat,Centralized kitchen is becoming very demanding, Tamil Nadu is still more focused on Decentralized mechanism.

PROFILE OF TAMIL NADU

The literacy rate in the state is close to 80% which is above the national average and that is something the state has worked on. The statistics in the Tamil Nadu Census 2011 reveal facts that can be taken into consideration by the government. The sex ratio in the state stands at 995 which is a big positive as the number exceeds the national average. Tamil Nadu covers an area of 130,058 km2 (50,216 sqmi), and is the 10th largest state in India. Tamil Nadu is mostly dependent on monsoon rains and thereby is prone to droughts when the monsoons fail.

In the 2011 census, Tamil Nadu had a population of 72,147,030. The sex ratio of the state is 995 with 36,137,975 male and 36,009,055 female. There are a total of 23,166,721 households. The total children under the age of 6 are 7,423,832. A total of 14,438,445 people constituting 20.01 percent of the total population belonged to scheduled castes (SC) and 794,697 people constituting 1.10 percent of the population belonged to scheduled tribes (ST). The life expectancy at birth for male is 65.2 years and for females it is 67.6 years.

IMPLEMENTATION MECHANISM OF TAMIL NADU

In Tamil Nadu, the implementation of scheme is taken care by Social Welfare and Nutritious Meal Program department. To addmore effectiveness,the state of Tamil Nadu has taken few initiatives, such as variety rice scheme, training program on Nutrition, health and personal hygiene, internal monitoring and involvement of Panchayati Raj Institutions at the village level committee to monitor the program.

PROFILE OF GUJARAT

As per 2011census, Gujarat has population of 6.04 crores. The literacy rate in the state is about 79.31%. Of that, male literacy stands at 83.23% while female literacy is at 70.73%. In the stateMid Day meal scheme is being implemented since 1982. Currently most part of Gujarat follows centralized kitchen mechanism under Public Private Partnership (PPP) for the implementation of Mid Day Meal Scheme.

IMPLEMENTATION MECHANISM INGUJARAT

In Gujarat, a separate Directorate for Mid-Day-Meal Program, has been established to effectively monitor the implementation and functioning of the programme.There are various schemes and initiatives provisioned for mid–day meals to the Children: like MDM trust,Building Public Private Partnership, Baal JeemanYojna, Annapurna Women Co-Operative Society (AMSS), School Development Management Committee and Schools adopted by private Companies.

3.4.6 SAMPLE PROCEDURE

Figure 10: Sample Framework

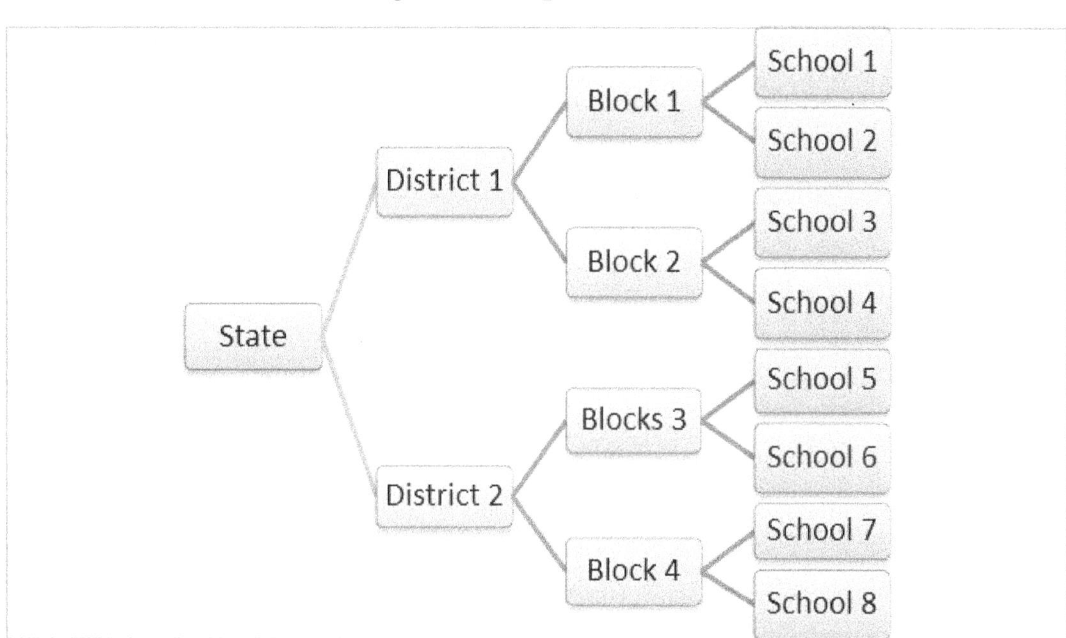

3.4.7 SAMPLE COVERAGE

In firth stage, two districts were selected and from each district two blocks were selected purposively from both the states. Two schools from each block were selected randomly. Per school 1 headmaster, 2 teacher and 10 students were randomly selected. Overall, 16 government /government Aided schools was selected from both the states. In Gujarat, centralized kitchen was observed, and in Tamil Nadu, the decentralized kitchen practices were observed. Total 160 students, 32 teachers, 16 principal from 16 schools from both the states were interviewed during the data collection. List of selected schools are attached in annexes.

Table 3: Sample Distribution

State	Districts	Block	No of schools	No of principal/ Head master(8*1)	No of teachers (4*2)	No of students (4*10)	Total
Tamil Nadu	1	2	4	4	8	40	
Tamil Nadu	1	2	4	4	8	40	
Total	2	4	8	8	16	80	118

State	Districts	Block	No of schools	No of principal/ Head master(8*1)	No of teachers (4*2)	No of students (4*10)	Total
Gujarat	1	2	4	4	8	40	
Gujarat	1	2	4	4	8	40	
Total	2	4	8	8	16	80	118
Grand Total	4	8	16	16	32	160	236

3.4.8 TARGET POPULATION

For the present study, to assess the information related to practices, challenges and perceptions towards Mid Day meal scheme the target population was all the stakeholders involved in the implementation process, like officials at district and state level (In charges of Mid Day Meal from Primary and Elementary Government schools),NGO partners, Block level officers, School Management Committee members, head of the school, teacher, students, parents and MDM staffs.

3.4.9 TOOL AND TECHNIQUES

Primary data was collected by using interview and observation schedule. Record/document analysis was done with the help of relevant secondary data like, policy documents, Annual Work Plan and Budget, MDM data, office orders and reports, mid day meal register at school level, pass book, check book, reconciliation book. These documents were collected from the Office of the Mid-Day Meal and schools. All related tools attached in annexes.

a. In-depth Interview schedule for stakeholders

At state/district/block/panchayat level officials of the Mid Day Meals, NGO partners were interviewed to collect information on Mid Day Meals Programme. At village and school level, Principal, teachers, students, parents and other mid day meal in-charge and staff were interviewed. Information related to the programme, their involvement, challenges and their perception towards current implementation process were collected accordingly.

b. Observation schedule at school level

Observation schedule was also incorporated to observe the condition of infrastructure available in both the models (Centralized and decentralized kitchen). For example- stores where grain is stored, kitchen-shed, cooking utensils and ventilation, availability of drinking water facilities, availability of water and for cooking and cleaning vessels, preparation and distribution of the meal, manners of children during the time of serving MDMS and hygiene conditions in school premises. Records books, number of cooks etc were collected from the headmasters and teachers.

Figure 11: Stakeholders interviewed at different levels

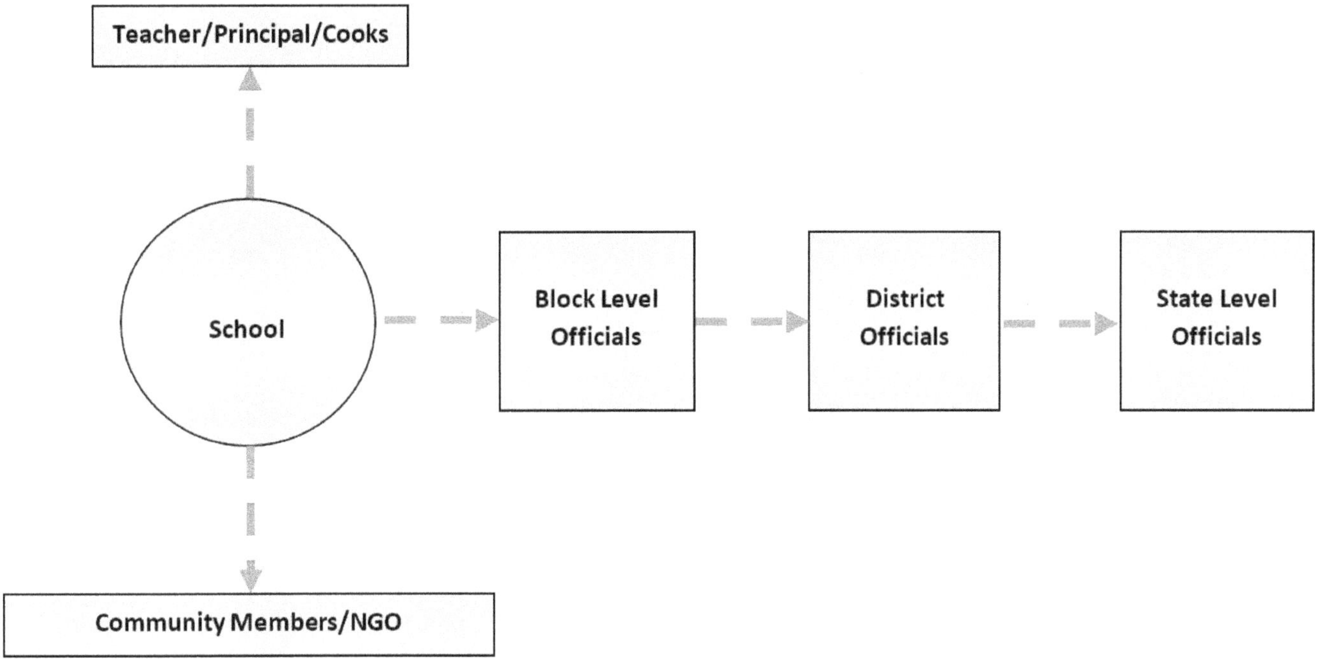

Table 4: Outline for collecting data using techniques from stakeholders involved at different level

States	Stages	Data	Type of Stakeholders	Tools/ Technique
Gujarat	State level	Primary data	Director-(mid day meal-directorate), NGO partners	In-depth interview
		Secondary data	Annual Work Plan and Budget, MDM data, guidelines for Mid-day Meal Scheme, and office orders and reports	
	District level	Primary data	Zilaparishad (C.E.O), NGO partners	In-depth interview
	Block level	Primary data	Block elementary education officer, NGO partners	In-depth interview
	School level	Primary data	Principal/teachers/students/parents/ MDM staff	In-depth interview
	School level	Secondary data	MDM account/Pass book/Check book/ Reconciliation account book/appointment letter	
	School level	Primary data	To note the condition and infrastructure available	observational schedule

States	Stages		Stakeholders	Tools/ Technique
Tamil Nadu	State level	Primary data	Director/Joint Director(SW/NMP Department)	In-depth interview
		Secondary data	Annual Work Plan and Budget, MDM data, guidelines for Mid-day Meal Scheme, and office orders and reports	
	District level	Primary data	Assistant Director/District collector	In-depth interview
	Block level	Primary data	Block development officer	In depth interview
	School level	Primary data	Organiser/cook/cook assistant	In-depth interview
	School level	Primary data	Principal/teachers/students/parents	In-depth interview
		Secondary data	MDM account/Pass book/Check book/ Reconciliation account book/appointment letter	
	School level	Primary data	To note the condition and infrastructure available	observational schedule

3.4.10 IMPLICATION OF THE RESEARCH

We all know that MDMS has a huge impact on education advancement, nutrition, social and gender equity and is one of the largest welfare programs in India. Therefore to make it more effective and sustainable, it is important to assess key welfare and hunger schemes. This study helps us to understand the governance framework and guided us towards new strategy which will work best and will be most effective in reaching the beneficiaries.

3.4.11 ETHICAL CONSIDERATION

While collecting data and information from schools and other department prior approval was taken by senior authorities. Prior consent was taken from the respondents before participation.

CHAPTER IV

MID DAY MEAL SCHEME (*POLICY FRAMEWORK*)

This chapter elaborates the evolution of scheme that took place during the duration of more than twenty years. On the basis of secondary data, policy documents and reports this chapter discussed how the situation demands for a policy, how it is being implemented. Why there was a need to keep on modifying the process and also introduction of new mechanism while execution.

In India, this need was recognized long back, and the first demand for education after Independence was that of Universal Elementary Education. The universalisation of elementary education was nationally accepted as an important aspect of the overall effort to make education a tool for socio-economic transformation. Article 45 of the Constitution also laid down that "the state shall endeavor to provide within of 10 years from the commencement of this constitution for the free and compulsory education to all children until they complete the age of 14 years."

Accordingly, in the post independence era the country has made giant strides in the provision of educational facilities at all levels especially at the 'primary 'level'. Primary level means suggest that it caters to the most fundamental needs of all individuals and without it no individual can do anything. This chapter mainly focused on the evolution of Mid Day Meal Scheme. How this concept emerged, years of transformation and challenges faced has been discussed in detail.

4.2 COMMISSION REPORTS AND POLICY DOCUMENTS

4.2.1 The Kothari Commission (1966) has envisaged "what is expected is that the primary education should lay the foundation for a child to grow into a responsible and useful citizen of country" (P.151). The report of the Indian education commission constituted in 1964 was a landmark in India education and history. This commission examined the role and goals of education in the process of national development. While dealing with educational factors responsible for wastage in school education, it included the following: (i) the dull character of most of the schools and their poor capacity to attract students and retain them; (ii) the absence of auxiliary services like school meals and school health; and (iii) the failure of the average parent to see the advantage of attendance.

The commission recommended organisation for a nationwide programme of 'school improvement while it commended the good work done in this respect in the Madras state where 'school improvement conferences' have been organized for some years and, large scale assistance from the **local community** has been obtained for improving school facilities.

The commission further recommended that there should be a School Committee to look after every government or local authority school in a given area. Half the members of these committees should be elected by the local authority in charge of the area, Village Panchayat or Municipality, and the remaining should be persons interested in education, nominated by the District School Board. This Committee would operate the school fund and will be responsible for arranging various facilities inclusive of the supply of Mid-Day Meals, besides performing functions related to school management. The resolution on National Policy on Education (NPE) 1968 declared," Strenuous effort should be made for the early fulfillment of the Directive Principles under Article 45 of the constitution seeking to provide free and compulsory education for all children up-to the age 14. Suitable program should be developed to reduce the prevailing wastage and stagnation in school and to ensure that every child who is enrolled in school, successfully completes the prescribed course."

The NPE (1968) emphasized equalization of educational opportunity through several measures such as correcting regional imbalances in providing facilities to rural and backward areas, girls and children of backward classes and tribal people, the children with special needs.

4.2.2 The National Policy of Education (1968), suggested a nationwide programme of school improvement commending the good work of Madras states in this regards. The provision of school health services, inclusive of school meal was viewed important. The policy accepted the recommendations of the school health committee under the chairmanship of Smt. Renuka Ray. The policy endorsed the Education Commission (1964-66) recommendation in the matter of constituting the school committee for every area and entrusting various functions relating to school education, exclusive management of school fund. Therefore, the school committee would organize and manage the Mid-Day Meal programme and enlist local support for its activities. 'The challenge of Education- A Policy perspective '1985 the document of the Ministry of Human Resource Development served as the basis for a nationwide debate for facilitating the formulation of national policy on education 1986. It stresses the crucial role of UEE in reconfirming the importance of Article 45 under Directive principles of state Policy in the Constitution and the resolution on NPE 1968 in this respect. It observed that measures such as MDM, free uniform and textbook and even central assistance to the nine educationally backward states for the appointment of women teachers in single teacher schools, had not yield significant results yet.

4.2.3 The National Policy of Education (1986) emphasized the importance of UEE. The programme of Action 1986 mentioned that a comprehensive system of incentives and support services would be arranged for girls, SC, ST and children of weaker section of society. Only in the case of girls, it has mentioned explicitly that the incentive of MDM would be made available for increasing enrolment and retention of girls in schools.

Dealing with education of SC, ST and Other Backward Sections, it had mentioned, the scheme of incentives would be worked out in consultation with the state government. In this regard incentives such as free uniform, textbooks & stationery and scholarships were included. However, MDM was not so explicitly mentioned. The national policy of Education was adopted once again in 1992 with certain modifications and endorsed by the Parliament.

4.2.4 The POA (1992) emphasized the significance of UEE and IPE. For encouraging participation, it said, adequate incentives would be made available for the children of SC, ST and Other backward Sections and especially for girls in the form of scholarships, uniform, textbooks, stationery and Mid Day Meal. On 15th August 1995, to enhance the effectiveness and nutritional status of the school going the children, GOI launched National Program on Nutritional support to primary school going children.

4.2.5 In 2002 the Constitution of India was amended (86th amendment) to alter the provision of Article 45 of the Constitution (Rampal, 2005). It made the provision of free and compulsory education as fundamental rights and affirmed the old commitment of the state towards education of the citizens. The 86th amendment inserted a new Article -21A- which reads: 'the state shall provide free and compulsory education to all the children of the age group of 6 to 14 years, in the manner of the state may, by law, determined'.

4.2.6 The Tenth Plan (2002-2007) has laid adequate emphasis on Universalisation of Elementary Education (UEE) with a view to ensure completion of five year of primary schooling for children by 2007. The Tenth Plan is guided by five parameters in proving elementary education.

Universal Access: All children in 6-14 age groups should have access to primary school, upper primary schools or their alternative with in a walking distance of 1 to 3 km respectively.

Universal Enrolment: Enrolment of all children including girls, disabled children and children belonging to SCs and STs etc. in primary classes and provision of upper primary education for them.

Universal Retention: Universal retention in primary stage by 2007 and dropout rates to be reduced to less than 10 percent for grade VI-VIII by 2007.

Universal Achievement: Emphasizes the importance of quality aspects in all respects (content and process) to ensure reasonable out comes at the elementary level.

Equity: Bridge all gender and social gaps in enrolment, retention and learning achievement.

Monitorable Targets:for the first time the national Development Council has set 11 monitorable targets for the Tenth Plan and three of these pertain to education.

- All children in school by 2003 (extended to 2005-2006) and all children to complete 5 years of schooling by 2007

- Reducing in gender gap in literacy by at least 50 percent.

- Increasing functional literacy to 75 percent.

In order to fulfill the commitment of Government to provide and finance universalized quality basic education in the country, the Finance (No.2) Act 2004 has provided for a levy education cess @ 2 percent on major taxes including income tax and service tax. The proceeds of the cess are to be utilized for elementary education schemes of SarvaSikshaAbhiyan (SSA) and Mid Day Meal Scheme (MDMS). In MHRD, PrarambhikSikshaKosh –a Non-Lapsable Fund was created for crediting the education cess proceeds. Estimated yields of the cess during 2004-2005 and 2005-2006 respectively are Rs 5010 crore (Revised Expenditure) and Rs 6975 crore (Budget Expenditure).

4.3 SarvaSikshaAbhiyaan (SSA) initiated during the terminal year of the Ninth Plan on 1st April 2010. Under Article 21-A of the Constitution of India, the Right of Children to free and compulsory education (RTE) Act was launched. It confers that all the children of age group 6-14 yrs has their right to get education. All the states and UTs have notified their State RTE system. It was decided that the fund sharing pattern between centre and state stands ratio of 60:40 between the centre and the state and 90:10 for 8 North-eastern states and in case of UTs, 100 % funded by Central Government .The fund sharing discussed in Table 13 was taken from (Two Hundred Eighty Report, Demand for Grants 2016-17[Demand No 51] of the Department of School Education and Literacy [MHRD], p.12, 2016)

Table 5: Fund released by the Central Government to State/UTs during the 12th Plan

Year	Budget Expenditure	Revised Expenditure	GOI Releases	% of GOI Releases to the RE
2012-2013	25555.00	23875.83	23836.55	99.84
2013-2014	27258.00	26608.01	24735.09	92.96
2014-2015	28258.00	24380.00	24030.16	98.57
2015-2016	22000.00	22000.00	19187.50	87.22

Adapted from "Two Hundred Eighty Report, Demand for Grants 2016-17", [Demand No 51] of the Department of School Education and Literacy [MHRD], p.12, Rajaya Sabha Secretariat, New Delhi, 2016)

4.3.1 PROGRAME INTERVENTION TO IMPROVE UNIVERSAL ACCESS

Accordingto report(Two Hundred Eighty Report, Demand for Grants 2016-17[Demand No 51] of the Department of School Education and Literacy [MHRD], 2016), 'Universal Access: within the period from 1998-99 to 2014-15, there was a noticeable advancement in universal access to elementary education'p.13.

Table 6: Gross ratio for Access, enrolment, dropout and over all out of school children

	1998-99	2014-15
Gross Access ratio (Primary)	83%	99%
Gross Access Ratio (Upper Primary)	76%	98%
Gross enrolment ratio(Upper primary)	92%	100%
Gross enrolment ratio (Primary)	58%	91.24%
Dropout rate (Elementary)	57%	32.62%
Out of school children	134.6 lakhs (2005)	60.64 (2014)

Adapted from "Two Hundred Eighty Report, Demand for Grants 2016-17', [Demand No 51] of the Department of School Education and Literacy [MHRD], p.13, Rajaya Sabha Secretariat, New Delhi, 2016)

To improve universal access, a set of interventions are ongoing such as:

- Construction of new schools,

- Special Training for mainstreaming out of school children,

- Residential facilities,

- Transportation or escorts,

- Free Uniforms,

- Ensuring an eight year elementary education cycle

For bridging the Gender Gap in elementary education, various actions have been taken are such as: promoting Girls Education, Kastuba Gandhi BalikaVidyalaya, Digital Gender Atlas for Advancing Girls Education in India, SwachVidyalaya Initiative for separate girls's toilet, MahilaSamakhyaProgramme, Padhe Bharat Badhe Bharat, in 2015-2016, Free Textbook for Children, was made for providing text books to 8.51 crore children. On July 2015, RatriyaAvishkarAbhiyaan was launched by Dr A.P.J Kalam.

4.3.3 INFRASTRUCTURE TO IMPROVE UNIVERSAL ACCESS

States are free to develop and design the infrastructure in school premises. There is no prescribed format on design and cost from the Centre. SSA adopts a school development approach for planning and construction.

4.4 HISTORICAL PERSPECTIVE OF MID DAY MEAL SCHEME

Mid Day Meal was basically launched toimprove enrolment, attendance and retention along with improvement on the nutritional status of school going children. Its genesis has a long history of initiatives spread across the sub-continent.

The report of the Committee on Mid Day meals **(1995)** dates the first step towards Mid Day Meals back in year 1925, when a MDM Program was introduced by the state Tamil Nadu for the children belongs from low socio economic group. A school lunch program was started in parts of state of Kerala in 1941, followed by

Bombay implementing a free mid day meal scheme in 1942. WHO with UNICEF assistance distributed skimmed milk powder to children aged between 6-13 years. Another project was launched in Bangalore city in 1946 where the scheme provided cooked Rice with Curd, to the children. The Uttar Pradesh Government introduced a voluntary scheme, in 1953 to provide meals consisting of boiled or roasted or sprouted grams, grounded nuts, puffed Rice, boiled potatoes or seasonal fruits. Several states introduced such schemes during 1950s, and with the aid of international agencies like UNICEF, FAO and WHO.

During **1958-59** an expand Nutrition Program (ENP) was introduced, funded jointly by FAO, WHO, UNICEF and Government of India. This was subsequently expended into the Applied Nutrition Program (Committee of Mid Day Meals, 1995). The idea of national Mid Day Meal Program was considered again and again for over a decade. In 1982, the idea of 'Food for learning' with FAO Commodity Assistance has proposed Scheduled Caste (SC) and Scheduled Tribe (ST) girls to be covered under this program. In 1983, the Department of Education under the Central Government after Inter-ministerial Consultation, prepared a scheme according to the guidelines of the World Food Program (WFP). The Scheme was to cover children 13.6 million SC and 10.09 million ST from class I-V in 15 states and 3 Union Territories where the enrolment of SC/ST girls was less than 79 percent. In monetary terms, the total annual cost of commodity assistance was $167.27 monthly. Other cost such as transportation, cooking, handling the food to be borne by the state Governments. The proposal was circulated among States and Union Territories with mixed results. While some states were willing to accept the scheme, other were skeptical. For instance, Rajasthan was concerned that in case WFP assistance was withdrawn, the state would not be able to continue the program on its own. Uttar Pradesh felt that it would not be practical to provide Mid Day Meals only for SC/ST.

During **1984-85**, a program with Central Government assistance for Mid Day Meal for the benefit of the children enrolled in primary schools across the country were considered. With the intention, that, the Mid Day Meal program for primary schools could form the basis of an anti poverty educational program. Secondly, implementation of this program for the children aged between 6-11 years may maximize enrolment and reduce school dropout rates, which were important for universalisation of elementary education as well as achievement of higher literacy rates in the country. In addition, this program would also help in providing nutrition to the underfed and under nourished children in rural areas.

The broader feature of the program was: Supplying of meals which provide 300 calories per day and 12-15g protein per child with coverage of primary school children in a phased manner. Expenditure per child per day including expenses on administration was 0.60 paisa. No elaborate administrative infrastructure was to be built up. Fund required for running the program to come from provisions marked for poverty alleviation scheme and finally, the States should arrange suitable logistics and make arrangements for cooks, helpers, administration, supervision and monitoring.

After **couple of years**, it was recognized that the scheme had some inherent problems such as such as possibilities of leakage, inadequacy of buildings, absence of teachers, participation by non school going children and misuse by those in charge of the program. It was expexted that these problems would get addressed with time. However the program was not approved as part of the subsequent annual plans, apparently due to resource constraints.

In December 1988, the Department of education formulated a proposal for covering 994 ICDS blocks with concentration of SC/ST children, @Rs. 1/- per child per day. The important element under this scheme was:

- The scheme should cover all children in primary classes in government and local body schools

- Mid Day Meals should be provided on all work

- CARE assistance, if any should be excluded

- Cereals and to the extent possible pulses, edible oils and condiments should be supplied to the schools through authorized states agencies.

In 1995, on 15th of August, this program was re- launched by our honorable Prime Minister of India and it was known as Mid Day Meal Program. The main focus was on increasing enrollment, attendance; reduce dropout and improving nutritional status of school going children. Universalisation of primary education being the National goal MDMP was launched with the following objectives.

- Increase enrolment, improve school attendance as well as retention

- Promote social integration

- Improve nutritional status of the primary school children

- Inculcate good food habit among children

The program envisaged the provision of cooked meals/processed food of calorific value equivalent to 100g of wheat/rice to the children studying in primary school. This recommendation was based on study done by NNMB (1990-92) on dietary consumption patterns of rural children using a one day 24 hour recall method. It was observed that the children had a deficit of the magnitude of 628 kcal and 6-7 g protein in the daily diets. From the nutritional gap of cereals, pulses, fat and vegetables, the cereal component could be the order of 60-90 % of the calorie deficit or roughly 100g of food grain/child/day.

The program which started on August 1995 spread to all India in 1997-98 and the coverage of children under increased from 3.4 crores in 1995-96 to 10.5 crores in 2003-04 in about the same number of schools. The coverage of more than 12 crore children in rural and urban areas under the scheme makes the Mid Day Meal program one of the largest nutrition support schemes in the world.

Initially it was perceived that the mode of delivery of nutritional support could be in the form of hot cooked meal, precooked food or food grains. Only four states viz. Gujarat, Kerala, Orissa and Tamil Nadu and the Union Territory of Pondicherry were providing cooked meals. All other states were providing dry rations supplied by Food Corporation of India (FCI) distributed under Public Distribution System (PDS) @Rs.3 per kg of food grain per child to a family for ten months which would be equivalent to set norms for 100g/day/child for 200 schools days (subject to a minimum attendance of 80 percent). Some states like Haryana and Kashmir reported that they could not implement the program due to resource constraints. Chandigarh and Delhi due to logistic problems continued to serve processed foods like fruit, bread and biscuits. Lakshadweep, which was implementing its own MDMP has been exempted from participating in the national program from 1997-98 as a special case.

The MDMP was implemented amazingly well in some states. The Pondicherry government has employed the state of art technology and has opened a centralized kitchen with latest food production gadget and sophisticated cooking techniques to ensure that meal cooked and are delivered to the children in a safe and hygienic manner. Each central kitchen was catering to about 8,000-10,000 children. Similarly, the Tamil Nadu Government has initiated a locally structured institutional machinery to ensure that the meals are delivered to the beneficiaries. Gujarat has an exclusive department overseeing the implementation of the scheme and has also been a pioneer in supplying fortified food to children. In Kerela, some teachers willingly contributed a portion of their salaries to ensure that conversion costs of raw to cook food are met and the food is served to children regularly. While the national Mid Day Meal program was being debated, a rather ironical situation was developing. Food procurement witnessed a quantum jump from 4 million tones to over 25 million per annum in two decades. This resulted in a sharp increase in buffer stocks in the warehouses of FCI with food stocks piling up to more than 3 times of what was required for food security. However at the same time deaths due to starvation in India was increasing. This state of affairs finally was challenged in May 2001 by a Public Interest Litigation filed by the people's Union for Civil Liberties, in the Indian Supreme Court.

The PIL argued that federal institutions and local state governments should, inter alia be responsible for mass malnutrition among the people. Jaishankar and Dreze (2005), "On November 28, 2001 the Supreme Court of India gave directive making it mandatory for the state government to provide cooked meals instead of dry rations. In one of its many directions in the litigation the Supreme Court directed the government to fully implement its scheme of providing cooked meals to all the children in primary schools"(p.3). S,Kaushal (2009) mentioned that, " the landmark direction converted the Mid–Day Meal scheme in to a legal entitlement, the violation of which can be taken up in the court of law. The direction and further follow up by the Supreme Court has been a major instrument in universalizing the scheme." (p.28).As mentioned in Supreme Court Order on 'Right to Food, A Tool for Action', Quotations from that order are: It is the case of the Union of India that has been full compliance with regard to the Mid Day Meal Scheme (MDMS). However, if any of the state gives a specific instance of non-compliance, the Union of India will do the needful within the framework of the scheme (p 31).Singh.G (2013), "The direction was to be implemented from June 2002, but was violated by most of the states. In May 2004 a new coalition government was formed at the Centre, which promised universal provision of cooked meals fully funded by the Centre" p(22). To achieve the promises done by the Centre, certain modification were done in Tenth Plan. It was suggested that the modification should be based on the feedback received from evaluation studies and opinion from the experts. The modification would include the following:

The program was expanded to cover children under Education Guarantee Scheme (EGS) and Alternative Innovation Education (AIE) and ending the present practice of distributing food grains and providing hot cooked meals or ready to eat food based on sound nutritional principles.

- Allowing adequate flexibility in the management of the program by the local bodies/ community through VECs, School management Committees (SMCs)

- Fostering strong community participation through Parent Teacher Association (PTA), and such other units of the school system in the implementation of the program. Encouraging the participation of credible NGOs, wherever possible

- Decentralizing the management of the program to reduce leakages and mismanagement.

- Providing funds in advance to the implementating agencies through State Nodal Officer for the transportation of food grains

- Limiting teacher's involvement in the program to supervision activities

- Extensive use of the computerized MIS (CMIS) for monitoring purposes. External agencies are to be involved in monitoring and supervision to ensure greater accountability. Elected representatives will also be involved in supervision.

- Linkage with poverty alleviation programs in rural and urban areas, adequate support of the Union Ministry of Health and State Health Department of Women and Child Development for nutrition and education.

4.5 PUBLIC PRIVATE PARTNERSHIP IN MID DAY MEAL SCHEME

In few states it has been seen that the Mid Day Meal Scheme got support with the interventions of Private and Corporate partnerships. This is an example of innovation in delivery of Public Services through the Private Partnership. In response to the difficulties of 'on -site feeding' a new focus on delivering an appropriately-timed (with regard to effecting improvements in learning capacity) and high quality, consistent ration, the government is developing program which include less costly commodities and most efficient systems for the delivery of meals to school children. Depending on the private sector and NGOs for the school feeding program helps in overcoming many difficulties of on site preparation of meals, and is one of the many inexpensive ways to feed children in schools. The private sector in this case could be a local canteen or caterers (in cities) or an NGO. An example of NGO and Central government partnership can be seen in Delhi and Bangalore where ISKON is supplying MDM in schools. After this experience, the education Department issued guidelines to facilitate participation by NGOs. Under the Guidelines State Government can select NGOs for the program, the food grains and transportation cost are provided to these NGOs who in turn take the responsibility of converting the grains into cooked meal. If we take the case of Akshaya Patra Foundation, the major allocation come from donation from big player in the market (National/International) and individuals in the city. This model has been successfully replicated few states including Gujarat. The program uses centralized automated kitchens for cooking meals which is then distributed to schools through special purpose vehicles. Akshaya Patra's kitchens can cook about 100,000 meals in less than five hours with least human intervention and sustained quality. A three items menu is served to children as per the recommendations of qualified nutritionists. The Akshaya Patra Foundation, joined world's largest school meal program and started serving school meals to student in Government schools of Ahmedabad and Gandinagar from mid 2007 onwards.

4.6 REVISION OF NP-NSPE IN 2006

During implementation of NP-NSPE, 2004, major difficulties were experienced. Therefore after two year of execution, revision of the policy took place in 2006. Following were the issues: as mention in the prescribed guidelines by (MHRD),2006, ' it has been decided to increase the amount of 1 Rs, as it was not fulfilling the cost of nutritious meal as recommended. It was seen that due to lack of proper kitchen food was prepared in open space, also the classroom was using as store room. As this practice damages the quality of food, kitchen shed and store room was proposed in revised guidelines. For growing children more nutrition is needed, therefore the prescribed calories/ protein found inadequate and was revised. In addition, essential micro nutrients and deworming medicines was recommended for better absorption of nutrition among children. For effective implementation strict monitoring is needed, therefore subcommittee was suggested at different level of the scheme.NSMC recommended increasing the calories intake i.e. 450g from 300g per student/day. Protein intake per child per day was also increased from 8-12g to a minimum of 12g. Adequate quantity of Micronutrient (Iron, Folic acid, Vitamin-A etc. for students that was not included in 2004 was also suggested in 2006. In the scheme FCI work as a nodal centre for delivery of free grain @ of 100g per child per day. It was suggested that the centre should provide cooking cost along with the area that is declared as drought affected to provide food during summer vacation.'p.15.

4.7 CONVERGENCE WITH OTHER DEVELOPMENT PROGRAM

Under the guidelines, (MHRD) 2006, 'It was decided in NP-NSPE **2006**, MDMS can be implemented with close convergence with several other development programs as detailed below so that all requirements of the program would be fully met in the shortest possible time frame'.p13. For example, constructing kitchen, there are scheme like basic services for urban poor, Sampooorna gram rozgar Yojana, sarvashiksha Abhiyan for constructing building. Regarding water supply, ministry of rural development, department of drinking water and for school health program, department of family and health welfare for routine health checkups.

4.8 INSTITUTION MANAGEMENT

According to the prescribed guidelines (MHRD 2006),envisages bringing in place the following management structures at the national, state, district /block and local level. At national level the Department of education and literacy has a setup of National Level Steering cum Monitoring committee to oversee the programe implementation. It also set up Proposal Aproval board under the Chairmanship of Secretary with membership of other respective departments. SarvaSikshaAbhiyan in addition assigned for time to time monitoring at national level. At state level, district and block involved in the process. In every state there is a nodal agency who took responsibility for implementing the project till grassroot level. The state in addition with central norms as per NP NSPE 2006, can have their own prescribed guidelines and referred as state norms. At distrct level the nodal agency ensure the delivery of the grains, financial sanctions also identify the transport agency through bidding. They have additional responsibility to develop nutritious Menu according to the resources available. As per guidelines the state is responsible for implementation of the scheme. State allocates local bodies such as panchayat, Parents –teacher association/ Village education committee/school development committee for day to day supervision at school level. The committee at local level can decide about the cook/ transportation of cooked meal etc.

4.9 QUALITY OF MID DAY MEAL

As mentioned by (Institute of food security) 2020,'theQuality of MDM largely depends on the quality of food grains. FCI is held responsible for issues with food grains if they are not of best available quality or not upto Fair Average Quality (DAQ). FCI appoints a Nodal Officer for each state to take care of various problems in supply of food grains under the MDM programme.' p.27.Accordingto the report(Two Hundred Eighty Report, Demand for Grants 2016-17[Demand No 51] of the Department of School Education and Literacy [MHRD], 2016)**,** 'In 12th plan, the Central Government has issued detailed guidelines to ensure quality, safety and hygiene under Mid-Day Meal Scheme to all the states/UTs.Mandatory tasting of the meal by 2-3 adults including at least one teacher before it is served to the children; Safe storage and supply of ingredients to school; procurement and supply of pulses and ingredients of Agmark quality on the lines of Maharashtra. The Detailed Guidelines on Food Safety and Hygiene for School Level Kitchens under Mid Day Meal were issued on 13.02.2015. These guidelines covered safety aspects of procurement, storage, preparation, serving and waste disposal of meals as well as issues related to personal hygiene of students and those involved in cooking and serving of Food'.p 36. Regarding information on which the policy development analyzed, reports suggested that in 2014-15 MDM-MIS has been launched with web enabled for getting better picture and transparency among stakeholders involved in the process. For better impact of the scheme emergency medical plan and grievance redressal mechanism was also initiated.

4.10 MONITORING MECHANISMS

As mentioned in the report(Two Hundred Eighty Report, Demand for Grants 2016-17[Demand No 51] of the Department of School Education and Literacy [MHRD], 2016)**,** 'Department of School Education and Literacy has prescribed a comprehensive and elaborate mechanism for monitoring and supervision of the Mid Day Meal Scheme. The Monitoring mechanism includes the following: Arrangement for local level monitoring, Display of Information, Block Level Committee, Inspection by state Government Officers, District Level Committee, Periodic Returns, Monitoring by institution of Social Sciences Research, Grievance Redressal, State level Monitoring, National Level Monitoring'.p35.

Joint Review Missions

As mentioned by MHRD in Annual Report (2014-2015), 'Headed by Nutritional Experts/Professor of Home Science University/Colleges consisting representatives of Ministry of HRD, representative from State Government, UNICEF, Office of Supreme Court Commissioner and Nodal officers from Monitoring Institutions have visited 46 states/UTS till 2014-15. In each State, 2 Districts were covered to assess nutritional indicators and actual indicators and implementation of the scheme at the ground level as per the defined Terms of Reference (ToRs). The report prepared by the Mission was shared with the concerned States for taking corrective action on the deficiencies reported in the implementation of the scheme and sending action taken note on the report. The collection of anthropometric data relating to Body Mass Index (BMI), level of malnutrition, stunting, wasting etc. was collected for the first time. These become a data base for measuring the impact of nutrition support under Mid Day Meal on children'.p.36.

Social Audit

As mentioned by Afridi,F&Iversen,V.(2013),in Discussion Report, 'MHRD facilitated the Government of Andhra Pradesh to conduct social audit on MDMS on pilot basis in two districts by Society for Social Audit Accountability and Transparency (SSAAT), Hyderabad during 2012-2013. To scale up this process in other States, a National Workshop on Social Audit was held in New Delhi on the 25th July, 2013. Thereafter Social Audit was conducted in two districts each on pilot basis in 9 States viz. Bihar, Karnataka, Madhya Pradesh, Maharastra, Odisha, Punjab, Rajasthan, Tamil Nadu and Uttar Pradesh'p.10.

4.11 CAPACITY BUILDING

Most important role in MDMS is of the person who prepares food for the beneficiaries. Therefore the up gradation of their knowledge and skill is needed. Henceforth regular training on personal hygiene, safety measure, healthy recipes, serving skill etc is needed. As mentioned in MHRD Anuual Report (2014-2015), 'MHRD has accordingly assigned the task of conducting the training of cook-cum-helpers in collaboration with Hotel management Institution, Food Craft Institution and Food and Nutrition Institutes in the State Agricultural Universities'. p.37.

4.12 NORMS FOR MID DAY MEAL SCHEME

As mentioned in the report(Two Hundred Eighty Report, Demand for Grants 2016-17[Demand No 51] of the Department of School Education and Literacy [MHRD], 2016), 'For children of primary classes, a cooked mid-day-meal consists of 100 grams of food grain (rice/wheat/nutria-rich cereals) 20 grams of pulses, 50 grams of vegetables and 5 grams of oil/fat to children which provides 450 calories of energy and 12 grams of protein. For children of upper primary classes, it consists of 150 grams of food grains (wheat/rice/nutria-rich cereals), 30 grams of pulses, 75 grams of vegetables and 7.5 grams of oil/fat which provides 700 calories of energy and 20 grams of proteins. Cooking cost covers expenditure on pulses, vegetables, cooking oils, condiments, fuel etc. The cooking cost has been increased by 7.5% in the last 5 years. The cooking cost is shared between the Centre and the NER States and Himalayan States on 90:10 basis, 100% for UTs and with other States on 60:40 basis. One cook-cum helper can be engaged for up-to 25 student's strength, two cook-cum-helper for schools with 26 to 100 students and one additional cook-cum-helper for every addition of up to 100 students. Each of them is entitled to a minimum honorarium of 1000 per month. The state are however free to give more honorarium over and above the prescribed minimum to the cook cum helpers from their own sources. The expenditure towards honorarium of cook cum helpers is shared between the Centre and the NER States and Himalayan

States on 90:10 basis, 100% for UTs and with other States on 60:40 basis. Program Approval Board of Mid Day Meal headed by Secretary, School Education & Literacy has approved the engagement of 27.39 lakh cook cum Helpers under the scheme. The State/UTs have engaged 25.75 lakhs cook cum helpers against the approval.The Center Assistance is being released to the State/UTs for the construction of kitchen-cum-store on the basis of plinth area norms and State Schedule of rate prevalent in the State/UTs. The Department has prescribed 20 sq. mt plinth area for construction of kitchen cum store in schools upto strength of 100 children. For every addition of up-to 100 children, additional 4 sq.mt plinth area is added. States/UTs have the flexibility to modify the slab of 100 children depending on the local conditions. The cost of construction of kitchen cum stores is shared between the Centre and NER States on 60:40 basis. Central Assistance of 8028.48 crores has been released to the States/UTs for construction of 10, 06,263 kitchens cum stores since 2006-2007. Out of this 7, 33,270 (73%) kitchen cum stores have been constructed and 1, 37,725 (13%) are under construction'.p.32.

4.13 COVERAGE

Accordingto report(Two Hundred Eighty Report, Demand for Grants 2016-17[Demand No 51] of the Department of School Education and Literacy [MHRD], 2016)**,** 'During the year 2014-2015, 10.22 crore children studying in elementary classes in 11.56 lakh eligible schools in the country were covered under the scheme. 25.57 lakhs cook-cum-helpers are working in Mid Day Meal Scheme and more than 80% are women. The approved outlay of the scheme during Eleventh Five year Plan was 48,000 crore against which 38,490.91 crores were released. The Planning Commission had approved 90,155.00 crores for the scheme during the Twelfth Plan. The Budget Estimates 2014-15 was 13,215.00 crores against which an amount of 10,526.97 crores has been released in FY 2014-15. The Budget Estimated (BE) has been enhanced to 9700 crore, which is an enhancement of 463.6 crore'.p.23.

Table 7: Progress of the scheme within the period

Year	Enrolment	PAB Approval	Actual Coverage	Coverage as % of enrolment	Coverage as % of PAB Approval
2012-2013	14.25	10.97	10.68	75	97
2013-2014	13.85	11.01	10.80	78	98
2014-2015	13.58	10.85	10.22	75	95
2015-2016	13.42	10.56	10.20	76	97

Adapted from "Two Hundred Eighty Report, Demand for Grants 2016-17', [Demand No 51] of the Department of School Education and Literacy [MHRD], p.23, Rajaya Sabha Secretariat, New Delhi, 2016)

CHAPTER V

INSTITUTION CAPACITY AND COORDINATION

Institutional capacity define as the capacity of an institution to set and achieve social and economic goal, through knowledge, skill, systems, resources (human, technical and financial) and institutions'. This chapter attempts to identify the list and roles of stakeholders in supply chain of MDMS at different level as well as the administrative structure of implementation.

5.1 IDENTIFICATION OF STAKEHOLDERS

The stakeholders are referred to those individuals who have some involvement in the project /program, together with an assessment of the nature and degree of their interest and potential to influence the program outcome. Program stakeholders are individual or multiple individuals having specific roles in participatory activities relating to different stages of the program cycle for example; Identification, Planning, Implementation, Monitoring and Evaluation etc. The process of stakeholders mapping can be viewed from the perspective of risk management. Risk management is the identification, prioritization of the risk (defined in ISO 31000 as the effect of uncertainty on objectives) followed by coordinated and economical application of the resources to minimize, monitor and control the probability or impact of unfortunate events.[4]

Once the stakeholders have been identified, the next step is mapping or categorizing according to different levels of engagement. Mapping of the stakeholders is done according to the level of interest and influence. By influence, it means stakeholders have power in setting and modifying program requirement. On the other hand, interest means that stakeholders are affected by the program outcome but they do not have any power to influence program requirement. This power/ interest matrix has been used by many NGOs to determine the impact on the stakeholder in their project. It can also help in selecting proper communication approach for each stakeholder group. Henceforth, this model classifies stakeholders based on their power and interest in the program. It allocates the stakeholders to one of the categories:

- High power/ High interest

- High power/ low interest

- Low power/ high interest

- Low power/ low interest

Once stakeholders identified, we need to draw two dimensional matrix*and assign stakeholders to one of four categories.

---

4. Hubbard, Douglas (2009).The Failure of Risk Management: Why it Broken and How to Fix it. John Wiley & Sons. P.46.

Figure 12: Stakeholder mapping matrix

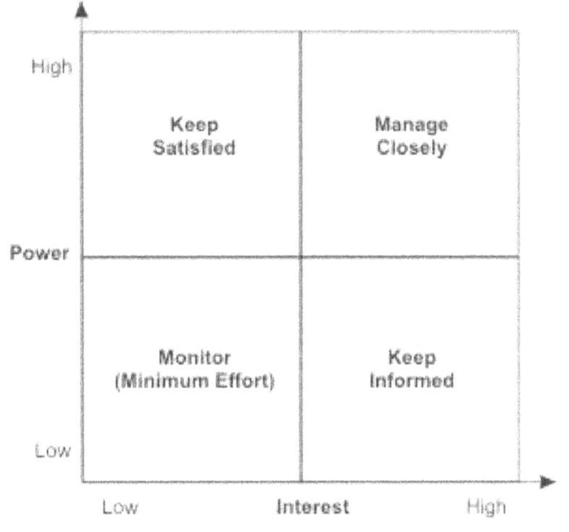

source stakeholders mapping Wikipedia image

Depending on the category, this model suggests different ways how to deal with these stakeholders. Stakeholders with high power and low interest shall be kept satisfied. Those with low interest and low power shall be involved with minimum effort, stakeholders with low power and high interest in a project shall be keeping informed and finally the high power and high interest shall be closely involved and informed. Once we have fully mapped the stakeholders, we need to create an action plan on their engagement. Mapping can be broken down into four phases:

1. Identifying: listing relevant groups, organization and people

2. Analyzing: understanding stakeholders perspectives and interest

3. Mapping: visualizing relationship to objectives and identifying issues

4. Prioritizing: ranking stakeholders relevance and identifying issues

In schemes like MDMs, which involve large number of stakeholders at different execution levels the process of mapping helps in identifying their requirement and managing their expectation. It also provides a visual tool to clarify and categorize the various stakeholders by drawing further pictures of what the stakeholders groups are, what interest they represent, the amount of power they possess, whether they represent inhibiting or supporting factors for the organization to realize its objectives, or methods in which they should be dealt with. It is very important to get them actively engaged in the program and to take ownership of the outcome of the scheme. Under Mid-Day Meal Scheme, stakeholders include government, suppliers, schools, NGOs etc at different levels ranging from national to regional/district to school. We can further separate into them into two sections which are internal and external stakeholders. Internal stakeholders are performing the key activities which are linked to flow of goods, funds and information, teachers, cook, children whereas, external stakeholders are linked with key activities such as linking food producers, trade, procurement, preparation and distribution, media etc.

5.2 INTERNAL STAKEHOLDERS

In any government sponsored scheme, all major regulation and guidelines are proposed centrally. They have major share in any scheme. In Mid Day Meal, both centre as well as state Government plays important role in implementation. Mid-Day Meal is a centrally sponsored scheme run by Ministry of Human Resource and Development at centre, which has proposed norms by which the states are regulated. India has 29 states with different culture, food habits, geographical terrain; the regulation helps in providing varieties of food by using best resources available, keeping in mind about the nutrition value and avail to the children. With the help of below Map we can figure out at what level who all are involved as a internal and external stakeholders as per guidelines.

Figure 13: Internal and External stakeholder Mapping

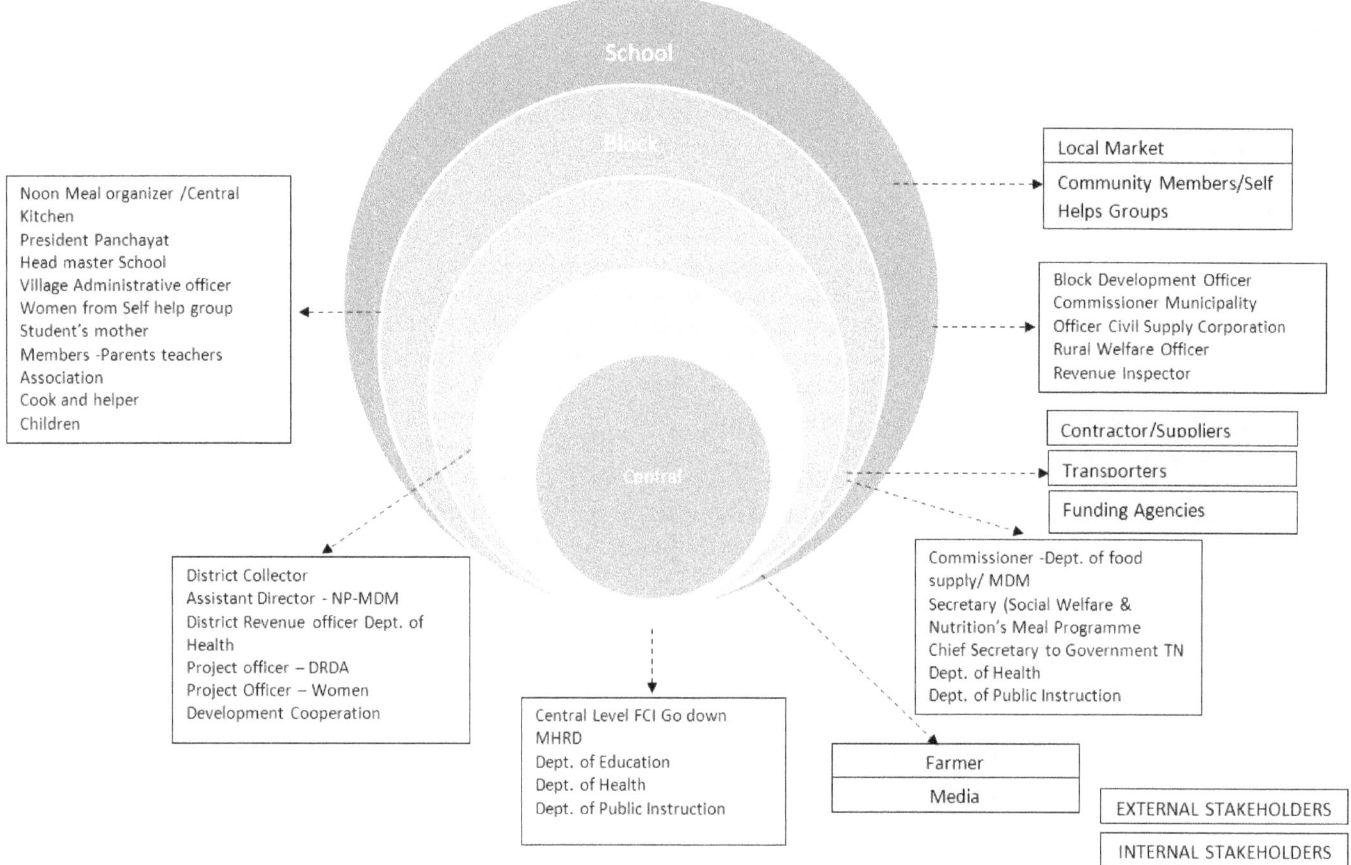

Table 8: At state levelagency/actors, department and their respective roles

Agency/Actors	Department	Key roles in MDMS
Commissioner	Department of food, civil supplies	Lifting and supplying food items float tenders and selections of contractors.
Secretary (Social Welfare & Nutrition's Meal Programme), Director (SWD) and Joint Director (NMP)	Social Welfare & Nutrition's Meal Programme Department	Implementing Mid-Day meal Program across the state
Chief secretary to Government, TN	State Government	Chairman of State level steering – cum -monitoring committee
Secretary	Social Welfare & Nutrition's Meal Programme Department	Member of State level steering- cum - monitoring committee
Secretary	Finance Department	Member of State level steering- cum - monitoring committee
Secretary	Planning, development and special initiative Department	Member of State level steering- cum - monitoring committee
Secretary	Co-operation, Food and Consumer Protection Department	Member of State level steering- cum - monitoring committee

Agency/Actors	Department	Key roles in MDMS
Secretary	Rural Development Department	Member of State level steering- cum - monitoring committee
Secretary	Municipal Administration and Weaker Supply Department	Member of State level steering- cum - monitoring committee
Secretary	School Education Department	Member of State level steering- cum - monitoring committee
State level officer	Food Corporation of India	Member of State level steering- cum - monitoring committee
Chairman and Managing Director	Tamil Nadu Civil Supplies Corporation	Member of State level steering- cum - monitoring committee
Director	Rural Development	Member of State level steering- cum - monitoring committee
Two expert in Nutrition		Member of State level steering- cum - monitoring committee
4 persons in the field of child development and district and teachers representatives		Member of State level steering- cum - monitoring committee
Treasurer office	Treasury Department	Deposition of fund at district level
Health worker(PHC)	Department of Health and family welfare	Provide supplements at district level

Table 9: At district level agency/actors, department and their respective roles

Agency/Actors	Department	Key roles in MDMS
District Collector		Chairman of steering - cum - monitoring committee, Personal Assistance (NMP) to Collector for Program operation at district and block level.
Assistant Director	Nutrition's Meal Programme Department	For implementation and monitoring of the program
Assistant Accounts Officer	NP-MDM	For accounts
Section superintendent (3Section)	NP-MDM	For implementation of the program
Assistants	NP-MDM	For implementation of the program
Data entry operators	NP-MDM	For implementation of the program
	NP-MDM	Member of District level steering - cum monitoring committee
District Revenue officer	Revenue Department	Member of District level steering - cum monitoring committee
Deputy Director	Grievance Day	Member of District level steering - cum monitoring committee
District Supply officer		Member of District level steering - cum monitoring committee
District Di-Dravidan Welfare Officer		Member of District level steering - cum monitoring committee

Agency/Actors	Department	Key roles in MDMS
District Backward Class Welfare Officer		Member of District level steering - cum monitoring committee
Assistant Commissioner	(Excise)	Member of District level steering - cum monitoring committee
Divisional Officers		Member of District level steering - cum monitoring committee
Revenue Tahsildar		Member of District level steering - cum monitoring committee
Taluk Supply Officer		Member of District level steering - cum monitoring committee
Project officer of	DRDA	Member of District level steering - cum monitoring committee
Project officer	Women Development Corporation	Member of District level steering - cum monitoring committee
Personal Assistance	PD to Collector	Member of District level steering - cum monitoring committee
Assistant Director	Parent Teacher Association	Member of District level steering - cum monitoring committee
Assistant Director	Audit	Member of District level steering - cum monitoring committee
Personal Assistant	(Noon Meal Programme) to Collector	Member of District level steering - cum monitoring committee
Joint Director	Medical	Member of District level steering - cum monitoring committee
Deputy Director	Health	Member of District level steering - cum monitoring committee
Corporation/ Municipal/Health Officer		Member of District level steering - cum monitoring committee
	District Rural Development Agency	Member of District level steering - cum monitoring committee
Assistant Project Officer	Women and Child Development	Member of District level steering - cum monitoring committee

Table 10: At block level agency/actors, department and their respective roles

Agency/Actors	Department	Key roles in MDMS
Block Development Officer		Chairman of Block level steering - cum monitoring committee and overall responsibility of implementation
Commissioner	Municipality	Look after fund
Officer	Tamil Nadu Civil Supply Corporation	Look after flow of grain
Deputy Block Development Officer		Member of Block level steering - cum monitoring committee

Agency/Actors	Department	Key roles in MDMS
Extension officer		Member of Block level steering - cum monitoring committee
Rural Welfare Officer		Member of Block level steering - cum monitoring committee
Revenue Inspector		Member of Block level steering - cum monitoring committee

Table 11: At Panchayat level agency/actors, department and their respective roles

Agency/Actors	Department	Key roles in MDMS
Officer	TNCSC Taluk godown	Supply grains and other commodities to school
Noon meal organizer	NMPD	Release fund for salary and purchase of vegetables, eggs, vessels, plates, tumblers and stationary
President	Panchayat	Panchayat Level Steering - cum- monitoring committee
Head master	School	Member – secretary
Village Administrative officer		Member of Panchayat Level Steering-cum-monitoring committee
Women from Self help group		Member of Panchayat Level Steering cum-monitoring committee
Student's mother		Member of Panchayat Level Steering cum-monitoring committee
Members	Parents teachers Association	Member of Panchayat Level Steering cum-monitoring committee
Cook and helper		Preparation of food
Children		Main stakeholders to whom the final product (meal) to be served

GUJARAT

In most of the urban and semi urban areas centralized kitchen system is in place where private institution or Non Government Organization takes the responsibility to cook and provide Mid-Day meals to schools. There are three main NGOs (Akshay Patra Foundation, Sri Shakti and Nayak Foundation) who are providing meals to the schools in the state.

Table 12: At state level agency/actors, department and their respective roles

Agency/Actors	Department	Key roles in MDMS
Manager	Gujarat state Civil Supply	Supply grains and other commodities to next level
Secretariat of Education department	School Education	Chairman of state level steering - cum - monitoring committee

Agency/Actors	Department	Key roles in MDMS
Commissioner	Mid-Day Meal	Member Secretary State Level Steering-cum- monitoring committee
Joint Commissioner	Mid-Day Meal	Member State Level Steering-cum-monitoring committee
Two Assistant Commissioners	Mid-Day Meal	Member State Level Steering-cum-monitoring committee
Secretary	Rural development	Member State Level Steering-cum-monitoring committee
Secretary	Urban Development	Member State Level Steering cum-monitoring committee
Secretary	Finance department	Member State Level Steering cum-monitoring committee
Secretary	Planning Commission	Member State Level Steering cum-monitoring committee
Secretary	Food and Civil Supply	Member State Level Steering cum-monitoring committee
Secretary	Women and child development	Member State Level Steering cum-monitoring committee
State Level officer	Food Corporation of India	Member State Level Steering cum-monitoring committee
Secretary	Health and family welfare	Member State Level Steering cum-monitoring committee
Secretary	Municipal Administration	Member State Level Steering cum-monitoring committee
Two expert of nutrition		Member State Level Steering cum-monitoring committee
Four) of two at least women) significant contrition		Member State Level Steering cum-monitoring committee
3-5 district representatives		Member State Level Steering cum-monitoring committee
1 teacher representatives		Member State Level Steering cum-monitoring committee

Table 13: At district level agency/actors, department and their respective roles

Agency/Actors	Department	Key roles in MDMS
District supply officer	Gujarat state Civil Supply	Supply grains and other commodities to Taluka
District collector/ municipal commissioner		Over all in charge of implementation and chairman of steering –cum- monitoring committee
Deputy collector/mamlatdar		Member secretary of steering –cum-monitoring committee
Deputy mamlatdar (administration)		Member of steering – cum- monitoring committee

Agency/Actors	Department	Key roles in MDMS
Deputy mamlatdar (inspection)		Member of steering – cum- monitoring committee
Deputy mamlatdar (accounts)		Member of steering – cum- monitoring committee
Account officer		Member of steering – cum- monitoring committee
Research officer		Member of steering – cum- monitoring committee
District development officer		Member of steering – cum- monitoring committee
District education officer (primary)		Member of steering – cum- monitoring committee
District supply officer		Member of steering – cum- monitoring committee
Chief district health officer		Member of steering – cum- monitoring committee
President municipality		Member of steering – cum- monitoring committee
Child welfare activist		Member of steering – cum- monitoring committee
Principal of home science		Member of steering – cum- monitoring committee
Sitting members of taluka		Member of steering – cum- monitoring committee
Teacher representatives		Member of steering – cum- monitoring committee

Table 14: At Taluka/block level agency/actors, department and their respective roles

Agency/Actors	Department	Key roles in MDMS
Taluka Mamlatdar		Overall in charge of the program and Chairman of steering –cum monitoring committee
Deputy Mamlatdar	Administration	Implementation of the program and secretary of steering –cum monitoring committee
Deputy Mamlatdar	Accounts	Implementation of the program secretary of steering –cum monitoring committee
Taluka Development officer		Member of steering – cum monitoring committee
Medical officer	Primary health centre	Member of steering – cum monitoring committee
Education inspector	Education department	Member of steering – cum monitoring committee

Agency/Actors	Department	Key roles in MDMS
Taluka Godown Manager		Member of steering – cum monitoring committee
President	Municipality	Member of steering – cum monitoring committee
Sarpanch		Member of steering – cum monitoring committee
Teacher		Member of steering – cum monitoring committee

Table 15: At school level agency/actors, department and their respective roles

Agency/Actors	Department	Key roles in MDMS
President	Gram panchayat	President of steering cum monitoring committee
Principal/ Head Master	School	Member –Secretary of steering cum monitoring committee
Organizer	Meal preparation	Member of steering cum monitoring committee
Four village prestigious persons out of which two women		Member of steering cum monitoring committee

5.3 EXTERNAL STAKEHOLDERS

Mid-Day Meal Scheme is a government driven program therefore active involvement of internal stakeholders can been seen i.e. government institutions at various levels, however there is an equally important role of external stakeholders in the supply chain for making the program successful and sustainable. List of external stakeholders and their roles in supply chain are identified as below:

Farmer: Technically, they are the strong base of this scheme. FCI is assigned as a nodal agency to collect wheat and rice in subsidized rate. The scheme is completely dependent on these farmers.

Neighbouring/ local marketplace: for daily consumption of vegetables and other ingredients the organisers purchase locally. Cooking gas is also supplied by the agencies selected at district level directly to the school.

Funding Agencies: The non for profit or charitable organizations receive fund and donations from various sources which is utilized to enhance quality of food they prepare for school children.

Suppliers: they are the one who are selected by state authority depending on their credentials for delivery pulses, oil, eggs and other ingredient.

Transporters: they are selected by the authorities to transport grains and rest of the items to the school or the centres.

Media: As per the Right to Information Act, public have the right to observe the process of grain supply and can seek any other information they want. In case of Tamil Nadu, the authority use this platform for communication recent updates directly and also ask suggestions from the community for any up gradation.

Parents /Community Member: As per guidelines there is a need of community participation for effectiveness of the scheme. Their awareness and their role and responsibility is equally important. Their involvement could be hiring cooks is done from the community, regular school visits are made to keep a tab on the quality meal served.

5.4 ADMINISTRATIVE STRUCTURE

As we know that MDMS is centrally sponsored scheme, therefore it is govern by the central government (MHRD). The norms and guidelines are made by MDRD that is further asked to all the states/UTs to implement accordingly. State government adapts the guidelines and implement across the state with the available resources. Central government had a tie-up with FCI for delivering grains to the respective states.

Figure 14: Administrative structure in Tamil Nadu

Figure 15: Administrative structure in Gujarat

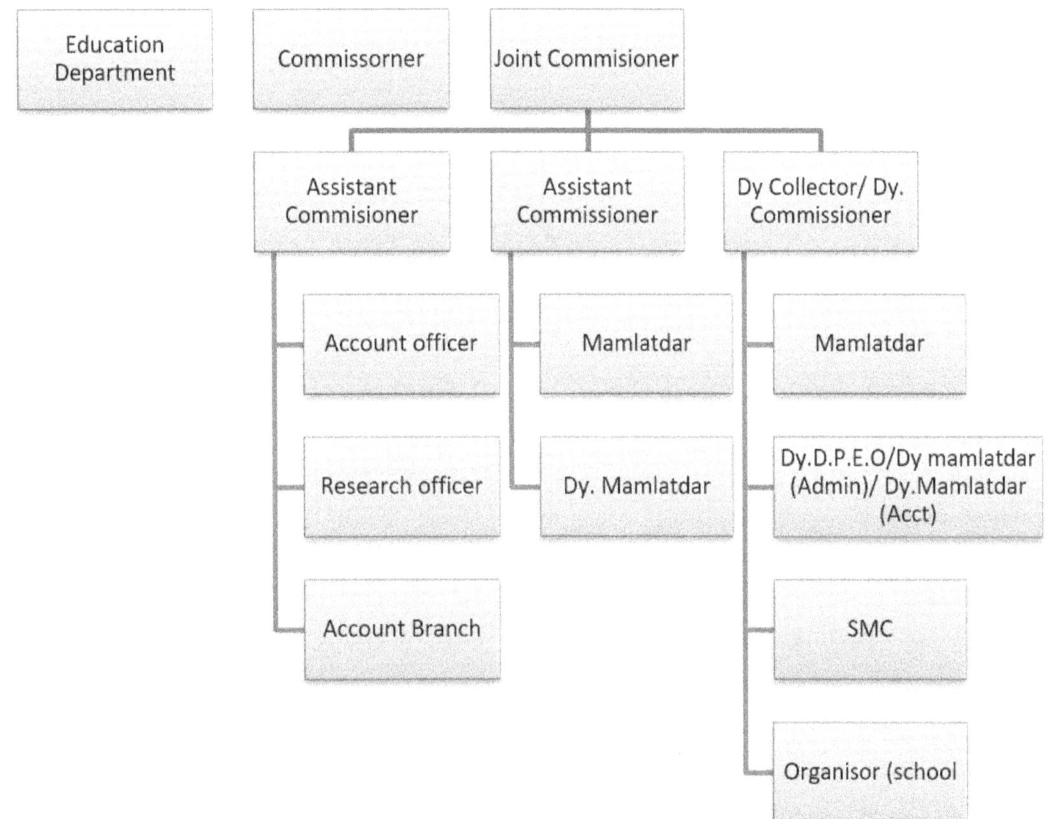

CHAPTER VI

DESIGN AND IMPLEMENTATION

This chapter tries to outline the activities involved in Supply Chain Process of Mid Day Meal Scheme that can enhance the implementation, impacts the efficiency and functioning of the scheme. Information gathered here is either by secondary sources or primary during interview with stakeholders involved in the scheme.

6.1 LIST OF ACTIVITIES

It refers process of covering flow of food grains and other important materials which helps in achieving the final product (hot cooked meal for the children). The various activities at different levels in Mid Day meal Scheme are as follows:

1. Trade and Procurement

2. Transportation & Distribution

3. Warehousing / Storage

4. Processing

5. Preparation of meals

6. Consumption

7. Resources

8. Oversights and quality control

6.2 CURRENT STATUS OF TRADE AND PROCUREMENT IN TAMIL NADU AND GUJARAT

It refers to food sourcing, buying and receipt of product. The aim of the procurement system is to ensure timely, uninterrupted supply of quality food grains for the Mid Day meal Scheme. This includes different set of activities to be undertaken to support the actual procurement. Usually this involves food procurement operating at different levels of aggregation throughout the school year. Trade refers to a market intermediation function between product supply and product demand. Multiple trades are possible between the original producer and delivery. In theory, each trade increases the value of the product. Increased value can include storage, transformation, packaging, preparation of any combination. Examples are, traders connecting farmers and caterers.

On the other hand, Procurement related activities includes: food procurement mechanism e.g. floating tenders, forward contracts, warehouse/storage receipt system etc., guidelines, procedures, tendering process, aggregation, quality control, market information systems, relaying data on demand from MDMS, adapting or creating regulations.

As per guideline Government of India allocated rice from Food Corporation of India and supply to the states. Based on the monthly advance intent, the TNCSC delivered items like rice, pulses such as (Toor Dhal, black Bengal and Green Gram,) oil to cook, Double Fortified Salt to the noon Meal Centre. There is a process of selecting contractor for supplying salt, oil and Daal to the noon meal centre. Further the purchase of vegetables, condiments, fuel etc Central Government provides required funds to the state regularly. Separate account is made and can be accessed by the organizer for purchasing rest of the things such as vegetables, fuel, cooking gas etc. Once in every three months Block level Officer release grant directly to the bank account of organizer.

In Gujarat, Civil Supply Corporation is entitled for the procurement. Based on food grain allocation letter from MHRD state office allocates food grains to district. District offices issues release order (R.O) to district godown manager of GSCSC for lifting of food grains from FCI godown every quarter. For ensuring lifting of fair average quality of food grains, deputy mamlatdar from district offices does joint inspection with district godown manager of GSCSC. In Gujarat pulses and oil are provided centrally by Gujarat Civil Supply Corporation Ltd and distributed to MDM centers. The state provides Rs. 2.38 and Rs 3.56 for vegetables, fuel, salt and condiments which are procured locally by helper of MDM centre. The Union Cabinet has taken a decision to purchase pulses for the MDM from GOI the buffer stock available with DoCA/NAFED. Under letter of MDRD 29/12/2017, it was stated that as per the decision of the GOI, pulses will be supplied under the Mid Day Meal Scheme (MDMS) 'in kind' through NAFED. Therefore, Gujarat procured pulses directly from NAFED.School Management Committee has been authorized to purchase the kitchen devices as per requirement of the school. The Central Government has granted procurement of kitchen devices @Rs 5000/- per institution to the state. The funds are transferred/allocated to the school through Block Offices. The SMC purchases & maintains the kitchen devices as per their requirement. Government of Gujarat contributes for eating utensils. The utensils are also provided through community participation. Under SanjivaniYogana, Rs 90 crores were sanctioned in 2018-19, to provide pasteurized 200ml of milk in all non tribal developing blocks for 4.81 lakhs beneficiary in 26 blocks.

6.3 CURRENT STATUS OF TRANSPORTATION AND DISTRIBUTION OF GOODS, FUND AND INFORMATION IN TAMIL NADU AND GUJARAT

Transportation refers to the flow of food grains and other commodities to the next activity level (ground, air etc) covering all stages from national/ state/district /block/ school level. Similarly money flows refers to the financial transaction in Mid Day Meal Supply Chain while the information flowsrefers to the exchange of information between supply chain actors. For example: enrollment figures from schools to program office in order to determine budget and food quantities, feedback between the beneficiaries and the program staff on the quality of service delivery, ordering information, providing guidelines, rules or other implementation support material etc.

In Tamil Nadu, calculation of total requirement of rice is depending on the children who were benefitted last year plus 45 days additional stock. This calculation had been done in every end of the year mainly September. This information further conveyed to the centre to release the required quantity. The centre once allocated, the letter issued to FCI and Chennai corporate for further process. In Tamil Nadu, The Tamil Nadu Civil Supply Corporation is assigned as Nodal Agency to supply food commodities to noon meal centers. Further the purchase of vegetables, condiments, fuel etc Central Government provides required funds to the state regularly. Separate account is made and can be accessed by the organizer for purchasing rest of the things such as vegetables, fuel, cooking gas etc. Once in every three months Block level Officer release grant directly to the bank account of organizer.

At state level grains are stored in the TCSC godown. Further, TCSC lifts rice from its regional centre and supply commodities every month as per indents. TCSC weighs the rice bag received from FCI and if the weight is less than 50 kg, it adds the missing quantity in the rice bag and supplies accordingly. They have made a schedule/plan for delivering rice every month between dates 15th to 25th to the centres. In addition, to avoid distraction in case of emergency, they provide extra 45 days stock to the centres.

After lifting Rice from FCI by TNCSC, the bills are submitted to the respective districts by TNCSC. In respect of Chennai Corporation, payment is made including transport charge by Director of Social Welfare, settles the bill through Pay and accounts office to TNCSC.

In Tamil Nadu, boiled eggs are provided to children respective to their age group. The contractors who have been selected to deliver the eggs to the Block level offices. In case of Chennai they directly delivered to the centres. The organizer collects the eggs as per their requirement and charge transportation cost on per egg from BDO to centre. It has seen that Tamil Nadu is having the least number of intermediaries in supply chain of food grains from state nodal agency to school which reduces the chances of leakage and corruption.

In Gujarat, fund flow from the State till Block level is done through e-transfer of IFMS (Integrated Finance management System) ensuring timely availability of funds. The State government releases advance grants to districts for a smooth functioning of the scheme. The MDM sanchalak has the responsibility of transporting the food grains from FPS to respective schools. The central government provided funds for construction of kitchen-cum stores to the state government. The state government handovers this fund to the Sarva Sikha Abhiyan for the construction of kitchen cum stores. Government of Gujarat has initiated modernization of MDM Kitchens in 2015-2016. The work is undertaken through Sarva Shiksha Abhiyan and technical expertise is sought for selection of right kinds of input by Akshaya Patra. Modernization of 500 MDM kitchens was undertaken at the unit cost of 4.50 lakhs across schools within this period.

6.4 WAREHOUSE/ STORAGE IN TAMIL NADU AND GUJARAT

It refers to storage of food products over a period of time. Examples at various level of the supply chain are short term storage, storage by farmer after harvest, storage by traders, storage at regional/ district and at school level by caterers and school management committee. In Tamil Nadu, storage of food grains takes place at two levels, district and school level. Tamil Nadu Civil Supply Corporation plays an important role in storage and supply of food grains. TCSC lifts rice from its regional centers and supplies forward every month the grains/commodities as per requirement received by the Centers. In both the places 45 days extra stock stored whether school or go down. At school level there is separate room provided by the state government for storage as well as storage bins. The first in and first out method is applied at stores to maintain the quality of the grains/commodities throughout the period.

In Gujarat, to protect food grains from wastage due to pests, galvanized containers with capacity of 50 kg, 100 kg and 200 kg has been provided to all MDM centers by the state government. Every MDM center uses small plastic containers for safe storage of ingredients to avoid contaminants in kitchen.

6.5 PROCESSINGSTATUS IN TAMIL NADU AND GUJARAT

It refers to value adding processes such as milling, packaging, fumigation and pasteurization. An additional special process may be fortification with micronutrients. It is important to understand that throughout the supply chain, different levels of processing takes places. For example Delhi based company PEC Ltd, is a public sector enterprises under Ministry of Commerce and Industry/ Department of Commerce, central government. The company imports bulk quantity of RBD Palmolein from Malaysia / Indonesia. The imported oil is re-packed in small packets for marketing by private companies.TNCSC procure 1 liter packet of palmolein oil from this company for distribution in Noon Meal Centre. The packaging material contains details with set of standard instructions e.g. the oil is 'best before', use 'within' three months from the date of packaging.

For shielding rice, green gram, bengal gram which are rich source of protein, in the state of Tamil Nadu they are in practice of using air tight container, drying grains few times in sunlight, mixing Vasambu& Neem leaves in the storage bins/ containers for controlling from pest infestation. In addition, to avoid malpractices, TN has taken the initiative to stamping the eggs. Every month they have decided one color. They are food graded colors. This will help them in ensuring that they are not delivering old or expired eggs to the centres. To prevent goiter among children state government strictly order to use fortified salt for cooking.

In Gujarat, fortification of food grains is under pipeline. They have initiated few procedures in association with PATH, New Delhi and meetings have been conducted regarding the fortification process as on 2017. In addition to this, communication started with Gujarat Co-operative Milk Marketing Federation Ltd. (GCMMF-AMUL) for fortification of wheat and Rice but at present they are not supplying fortified wheat floor.

6.6 PREPARATION OF MEAL IN TAMIL NADU AND GUJARAT

It involves a set of activities generally undertaken to provide meals at school level. Activities include cooking of meals, preparing servings and it's distribution to the beneficiaries. The activities also include training of cooks to provide adequate quality of meals, fuel for cooking in kitchen, separate utensils for cooking, serving utensils and tableware. Cooks are trained to ensure hygiene and sanitation in kitchen e.g. kitchens equipped with fuel-efficient stoves, chimney as exhaust, and clean portable water. In Tamil Nadu, where more than 500 children study, one cook with assistant are recruited. One head organiser is also appointed who is overall incharge of the centre. His main job is coordination and arrangement. The organizer also maintains the record of MDM items supplied at the school. He supervises work of cook who prepares meals and his assistant who serves of meal.

At present, inGujarat, three NGOs namely Stri Shakti, Akshaya Patra Foundation &Nayak Foundation are serving cooked food under the MDM Scheme from their centralized kitchens in 7 districts, across 3327 schools. This entire centralized kitchen follows ISO 2200:2005 standards. Register under Factory Act and compliance as per FSSAI guidelines; comply with other Licenses and permission as per the requirement. Kitchen consists of different sections like full-fledged sweet, nankeen, bakery which are provided as additional items with the meal to the school children. The kitchen runs on steam generating boilers with capacity of 2000 kgs, 7 Stage rice cleaning machines, Roti making machines with capacity of 40,000 rotis/hour, Rice and Dal Silos, cold room, STP and RO Plants. All equipment & utensils used for cooking are sanitized every day before cooking by steam. Distribution of food is done through custom built vehicles in SS304 (Food Grade) vessels to maintain hygiene and the temperature. All vehicles are installed with a GPS system to track its movement and ensuring on time delivery. In house, food lab tests the quality of prepared meal, water, and other raw materials too. Maximum distance covered is 55km and the maximum time taken to delivery meal at school is 1-2 hr from the centralized kitchen.

6.7 CONSUMPTION OF FOOD IN TAMIL NADU AND GUJARAT

This scheme not only provides cooked food but also promotes discipline among the children. In Tamil Nadu, it is mandatory for the children to wash their plates and glasses before and after consuming meals, also they have maintain queue and wait for their chance patiently. During this study it was found that this scheme has developed an atmosphere of brotherhood among the children who sit below under one roof and have meals together without worrying about caste and class prejudice.

In Gujarat, food is delivered by centralized kitchen, hence the head teacher has the responsibility of ensuring hot cooked meals are delivered on time. Schools are supposed to have weighing machines for weighing food at the time of receiving from central kitchen. The maximum time taken in supply of meals to schools should be not more than 1 to 2 hrs and the tiffin boxes should be sealed. The labs at Food and Drugs Laboratory (Varodara), Ahmedabad Corporation and Rajkot are engaged in testing food made in centralized kitchen.

6.8 OVERSIGHT AND QUALITY CONTROL IN TAMIL NADU AND GUJARAT

It involves the monitoring and evaluation of program activities, including inputs, process, output and outcomes. For example, it includes the development and use of management information systems by the Ministry of education for betterment of the process. Further these activities include specific monitoring activities by ensuring the service delivery of mid day meal which should be timely and of adequate quality and quantity. Examples of quality control activities include monitoring of food quality, assessing food storage and preparation, testing for aflatoxin etc.

In Tamil Nadu, on regular intervals stakeholders (officials from different department) involved in the process visit to the centres and monitor. On the basis of their findings steps are taken to rectify the omission/defects then and there. During the fieldwork it was found that the records like cash book, attendance, stock register etc are fully maintained. Inspection done periodically by the officials. They also have visiting records about officials visited with their comments. Under the scheme, there is also a provision of social auditing to monitor the quality of food by the locals. It is conveyed by NMP officials to all the schools to taste the food half an hour before serving the food to the children and also has been asked them to maintain a taste register. In addition, all the Noon Meal Centers have been registered under the 'Food Safety and Standard Act'.

In Gujarat, in case of any delay in lifting of the food grains, the matter is resolved by Coordinator taking it up, with the concerned authorities immediately. As per GR of Department of Education dated 22/03/2011, responsibility of implementation of MDM scheme has been entrusted to SMC. Under the scheme the food grain is allocated to district offices quarterly as received from central government on the basis of number of children and number of school days approved by PAB of MDM. For the payment of food grains through district offices, this office ensures that adequate funds are available to districts and in monthly review meeting it is checked that if bills are being paid on time. Regular follow up is done with the district through video conference and collector conference for regular payment to FCI. Frequent meeting are organized at state and district level to address any delay related to payment issues. After receiving pending payment report from FCI, state office forwards this directly to the concerned districts to clear the bill in accordance with time limit. FCI submits the bill to district office through regular post and hence it reaches late to district offices. There have been instances when bills did not reached to the district offices or the cheques issued to FCI got lost at the regional offices of FCI. Such issues are reconciled through regular follow up.

Every MDM centers use First in and First out (FIFO) method for usage of pulses and condiments etc. In every schools teachers has been instructed to taste and also eat meal with school children on rotational basis. Instructions through Chief Secretary's letter has been given to all District Collector and Municipal Commissioners for a rigorous monitoring at the district level including sampling and testing of food grains and finished meals through accredited Labs. Engagement of NABL labs for the testing of meals has also been provisioned. The frequency of lifting and testing of samples is carried out twice in a year in every district. MDM Logo and weekly menu are displayed at every MDM centre. Information related to MDM is displayed on education department's website. The matter is widely discussed in SMC training for creating awareness among local stakeholders. Pamphlets covering information are distributed in large numbers to create awareness. The meeting of Gramsabha is held in every 3 months Gujarat State. Government of Gujarat has issued detailed instructions to conduct social audit of MDM by Gram Sabhas. In addition, Social Audit is also carried out by Mahatma Gandhi Labour Institute, Ahmedabad. Regular inspection is under taken by respective authorities in all the schools with various inspection formats. Deputy Collectors also send monthly reports in prescribed performa covering several of salient indicators. The Chief Secretary has instructed all the District Collectors to take up the inspection of MDM centres in a campaign mode. The same is compiled by district authority in a rigorous manner.

6.9 RESOURCES AVAILABILITY AND ITS UTILIZATION IN TAMIL NADU AND GUJARAT

Resources include cash or kind support for program implementation and management (setting of guidelines and standards, monitoring and evaluation). Examples of resource transfer include financing through Ministry of finance and Community contribution (labor, fresh fruits etc).

The Central Government provides fund for implementing the program in the ratio (60:40) to states (centre: state). Accordingly, cooking cost & honorarium to cook cum helpers are shared by centre and state in the ratio (60:40), while purchase of food grains, transportation of food grains, monitoring management and its evaluation component is 100% funded by central government.

In Tamil Nadu, from class 1st to 8th food grains (rice) are provided by Central Government at the rate of Rs 5,650/- per MT. In addition, Central Government also provides Rs 750/- per MT for transporting rice from the nearest FCI godown. The state government has extended the program to class 9th and 10th children and the entire expenditure is covered under state funds. Rice for these children is supplied by TNCSC @RS 10,318/- per MT. Cooking cost (central share Rs 2.48 and state share Rs 1.65) for primary and Rs 6.18 (central share Rs 3.71 and state share Rs 2.47) for upper primary children. However the state provides more than the mandatory share of 40% (Primary children Rs 2.65 and Upper Primary Rs 0.70) to ensure nutritious meals are provided to children. Regarding kitchen cum store, central government contributes a share of 60 % of the construction cost and 40% is borne by the state. In order to create smokeless atmosphere in the noon meal centers, for modernization of noon meal centers, LPG connections have been provided exclusively from state funds. A sum of Rs 22,350/- has been provided per unit for providing gas connection, gas stove, construction of cooking platform, non returnable valve, safety measures etc. for kitchen devices Rs 5000 are provided by the centre. To meet the contingent expenditure such as purchase of cleaning material like soap, broomstick, phenyl etc, each noon meal centre is being provided with Rs 50 per month.

In year (2016-2017) there were 43,047 Noon Meal Centers catering 55.05 lakhs children studying from class I to X. Each Noon Meal Centre has three sanctioned post of Noon Meal Organizer, cook and cook Assistant. But if the number of beneficiaries exceeds in school, an additional cook assistant can be appointed. As per the norms of the Central Government only one post of cook cum helper is allowed at strength of 25 beneficiaries and an honorarium of Rs 1000/ is allowed in the sharing pattern of 60:40 between centre and state. The Government of Tamil Nadu, in order to provide quality, healthy, safe and delicious food for children, has provisioned for appointing three staff, namely organizer, Cook, Cook assistant in each centre. There are 1,28,130 sectioned post of Noon Meal Organizers, 42852 cooks and 42855 cook assistant in the year 2016-2017.

A state level steering cum monitoring committee under the chairmanship of chief secretary to government has been constituted by the state government. In addition District and Block level committees have been formed to review and monitor the progress of the scheme at respective levels. A special initiative, since 2013, for conducting Social Audit has been introduced to create awareness among the general public and to encourage committee participation. The accounts of the noon meal centre are placed before the Gram Sabha twice in a year (January 26th and August 15th), in which the students, teachers, mothers and public, participate actively and detailed discussion happens. Under management information system, the details are updated monthly to the Central Government covering data on children benefited under MDM, noon meal centers, kitchen cum store, gas connection, water facility, movement of supplies made from the TNCSC, bill raised and settled, details of cook cum helpers engaged etc., are uploaded in block and district levels.

In Gujarat, training has been provided to all cook cum helpers under the supervision of Principal Secretary, Commission of MDM, Gandhinagar, Senior Food Safety officers, CDPO from ICDS, deputy Collectors of MDM. The training has been given through SETCOM (BISEG). Content of the program mainly focuses on topics like health and cleanliness, preservation of raw material and hygienic condition, Guidelines for nutrition and food safety, cooking technique, financial and administrative matters and strategy for implementation. Mothers from the community are involved in monitoring and supervising Mid Day Meal in the schools. All account of MDM are regularly maintained and inspected at MDM centre, block, District and State Level. The State has issued instructions to every Dy. Collector to deduct Rs.12 for Pradhan mantrai Jan DhanYojana, Pradhan MantriSurakhsaYojana, Pradhan mantra Jeevan BeemaYojana etc. for honorarium of cook cum helper. Due to shortage of staff and vacant posts at State, District and Taluka level, monitoring system is facing challenges. It wasfound that recruitment of 310 MDM Supervisors was carried out and 234 MDM Supervisor were recruited for an effective and regular inspection of MDM. Automated Monitoring System (AMS) has been installed at school, block and at State level. From 1-07-2016 to 30-04-2017 data was collected through IVRS system, from 05-06-2017 onwards website/Mobile application is operational. At School level the head teacher has to update the daily status of meal served to students using the website login ID/mobile application interface. The daily reporting can be done between 7 am to 11 pm. AMS data is been monitored at the block level & state level through their respective unique login ID and password.

6.10 SUPPLYCHAIN FLOW OF GRAINS AND OTHER ITEMS

As per guideline Government of India allocated rice from Food Corporation of India and supply to the states. Based on the monthly advance intent, the TNCSC delivered items like rice, pulses such as (Toor Dhal, black Bengal and Green Gram,) oil to cook, Double Fortified Salt to the noon Meal Centre. There is a process of selecting contractor for supplying salt, oil and Daal to the noon meal centre. Further the purchase of vegetables, condiments, fuel etc Central Government provides required funds to the state regularly. In case of LPG, the Noon Meal Organizer buys it from the nearest Gas Agencies. The organizer also buys milk, sugar, vegetables and spices from local shop/ mandis on daily basis through contingency grant.The organiser collects eggs directly from the BDO.

Whereas in Gujarat, the Civil Supply Corporation (GSCSC) are assigned for the procurement. Based on food grain allocation letter from MHRD state office allocates the food grains to district based on respective beneficiaries. District offices issues release order (R.O) to district Go down manager of GSCSC for lifting of food grains from FCI godown every quarter. For ensuring lifting of fair average quality of food grains, deputy mamlatdar from district offices does joint inspection with district godown manager of GSCSC. In the State of Gujarat pulses and oil are provided centrally by Gujarat Civil Supply Corporation Ltd and distributed to MDM centre. The State provides Rs. 2.38 and Rs 3.56 for vegetables, fuel, salt and condiments which are procured locally by helper of MDM centre.

Figure 16: Supply chain of grains and other items

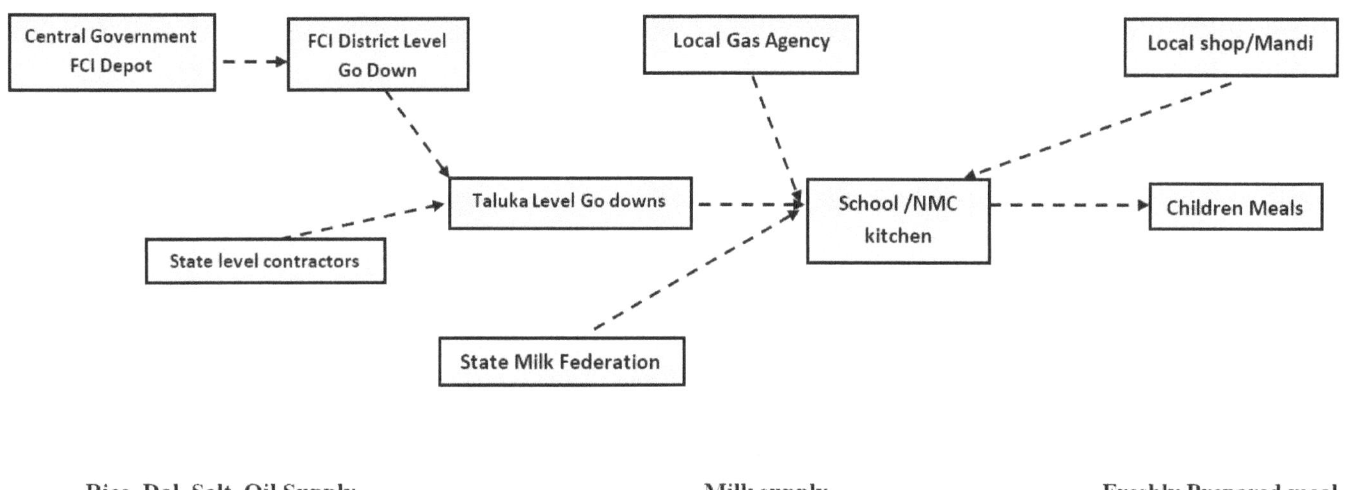

6.11 SUPPLY CHAIN FLOW OF FUNDS

Depending on the previous year beneficiaries, current budget plan prepared and was share with the central government. Once received the fund it was trasfered to the respective department. In case of TN it is transferred to the Social Welfare and Nutritious Meal Program Department, Commissioner (Municipal Administration) and Commissioner Civil Supply. They further e- transfer to District Collector at District level. At Block level, the fund is transferred by District Collector to Block Development officer, Municipality Commissioner and Tamil Nadu Civil Supply Corporation, utilizing for rice, daal, oil and salt. BDO and Municipality Commissioner further e-transfer to the Noon Meal Centres and from there Noon Meal Organizer takes funds under different expenses like Salary grant, purchase of vegetables, eggs, vessels, plates, tumblers and stationary. To avoid any distraction fund transferred with a period of 45 days.

The State provides Rs. 2.38 and Rs 3.56 for vegetables, fuel, salt and condiments which are procured locally by helper of MDM centre. The Union Cabinet has taken a decision to purchase pulses for the MDM from GOI buffer stock available with DoCA/NAFED. Under letter of MDRD 29/12/2017, it was stated that now as per the decision of the GOI, pulses will be supplied under the Mid Day Meal Scheme (MDMS) 'in kind' through NAFED. Therefore Gujarat procured pulses from directly from NAFED.School Management Committee has been authorized to purchase the kitchen devices as per requirement of the school. The Central Government has granted procurement of kitchen devices @Rs 5000/- per institution to the state. The funds are transferred/allocated to the School through Block Offices. The SMC purchase & maintains the kitchen devices as per their requirement. Government of Gujarat contributes for serving utensils. The utensils are also provided through community participation. The State of Gujarat provides cooking cost at the rate of Rs. 4.58 for Primary student and Rs 6.41 for Upper Primary students. The money is utilized for the purchase of vegetables, fuels, salt and condiments. Rest of cooking cost is given to Gujarat State Civil Supplies Corporation for purchase of pulses and oil.

Figure 17: Supply chain flow of funds

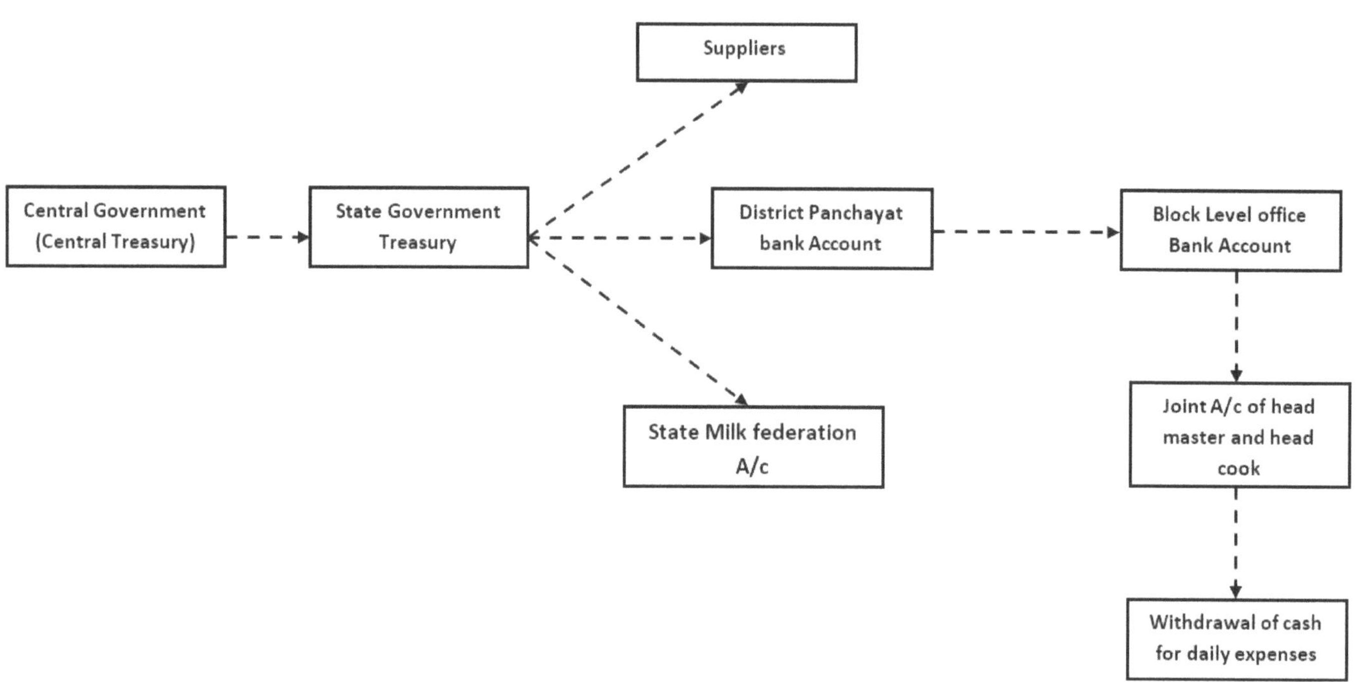

6.12 FLOW OF INFORMATION

Some information flows top to bottom where as some bottom to up. In case of MDMS the school provides required information to the block and then block officer forward it to the district officer. Through the tracking devises they get to know all the information related to grains and by the format received by the school they get information about the balance and the surplus left at the end of every month. Different records werefilling on MIS by block level officers on daily basis. This uploaded information further access by the district and state officer.

In Gujarat, Annual data and monthly data entry forms are filled up at school level and they are sent to block offices for data entry. Data entry is made both at block and district level. 31 district project coordinators are recruited on contractual basis for smooth functioning of web based MIS which is used for monitoring purpose. To ensure data entry and its quality, fortnightly meetings are held at block level and same is reviewed in monthly meetings at District and State level. Automated Monitoring System (AMS) has been implemented at school, block and State level. From 1-07-2016 to 30-04-2017 data was collected through IVRS system, thereafter from 05-06-2017 onwards website/Mobile application is operational. At School level the head teacher has to update the daily status of meal served to students using the website login ID/mobile application interface. The daily reporting can be done between 7 am to 11 pm. AMS data is been monitored at the block level & state level through their respective unique login ID and password.

Figure 18: Flow of information across different level

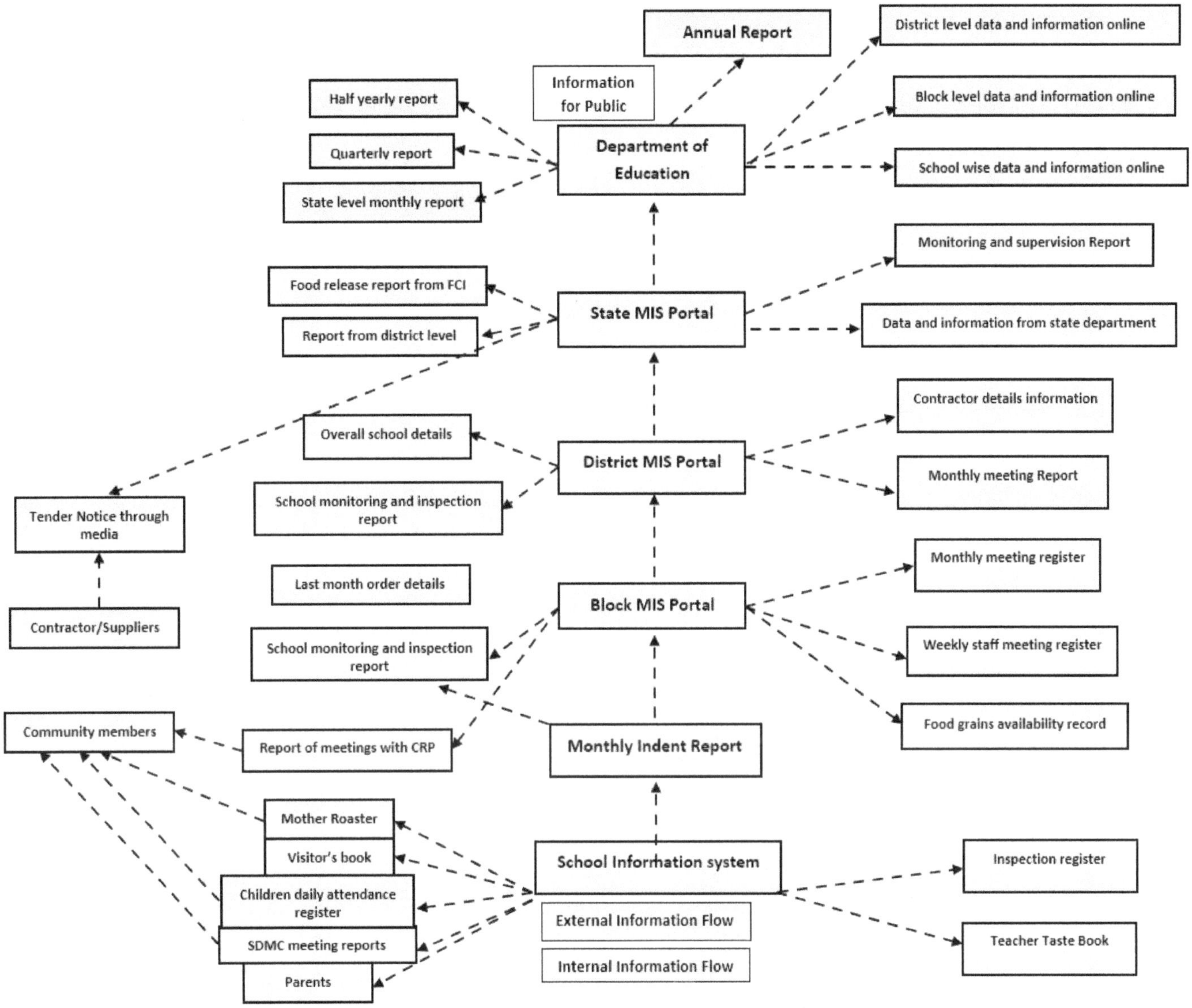

CHAPTER VII

ASSESMENT OF RISK & CHALLENGES IN MDM SUPPLY CHAIN PROCESS

Earlier chapter discussed about the list of activities in Mid Day Meal Scheme. While operating all those activities, there are scope of risks and challenges. This chapter tries to understand and identify the key potential problem areas that can arise in any stage in supply chain and may have an impact upon supply chain performance. It is very important to rectify such issues in early stage of programme planning, so that it cannot create hindrance while implementation.

7.1 BACKGROUND

Risk and challenges has been traditionally defined as possibility of danger, loss, injury or other consequences. According to the Committee of Sponsoring Organisation of the Thread way commission (COSO), Risk has been defined as, 'the possibility of event that can occur and adversely affect the objectives of the scheme'. Various organisations at National/International level have conducted detailed studies on Risk management[5] and proposed Risk Management Frameworkswhich provides the basic conceptual structure used to address the risks faced by anorganisation. Government of United Kingdom, New York State, Victorian and Finland along with private companies such as ITC, DLF, Dr.Reddy's Laboratories, Hindalco industries Ltd and Tata Metallic have adopted combinations of Risk Management Framework Standards and have been effectively managing the Risks inherent in their operations. Numbers of literatures have suggested that risk inculcates across all the organisations both in Government as well as Private Sector. In 2012, DARPG used Risk classification framework and conducted a pilot study on Mid-day meal scheme in Dungarpur District of Rajasthan,to identify key issues being faced by the implementation agencies. The main purpose of identifying the Risks and challenges was it will help at the time of conceptualization and implementation of the scheme.

According to World Bank framework, risk and challenges directly impact the functioning of food based supply chain. It also identified the Risk drivers that have an impact on food supply chain dimensions. And if we identify in supply chain, it will be helpful for appropriate implementation of the scheme.

---

5. INTOSAI Guidelines for Internal Control, Australia and New Zealand Standards 4360 :2004 and COSCO Enterprise Risk Management Framework

Figure 19: Risk and vulnerabilities

Source: World Bank Risk and Vulnerabilities Drivers

7.2 TAMIL NADU

In Tamil Nadu, Nutritious meal centers coveringschools in rural and urban areas under the administrative control of the Directorate of Social Welfare. The district officials belong to Rural Development Department who implement the program at District level.Regarding managerial and operational risk, the officials reported that, for providing nutritious food for children, Tamil Nadu issued guidelines to provide more than the mandatory share of 40% (Primary children Rs 2.65 and Upper Primary Rs 0.70). The state Government has also extended the program to 9th and 10th STD children and the entire expenditure is met by state funds. Rice for these children supplied by TNCSC @RS 10,318/- per MT. Along with hot nutritious meal Tamil Nadu also decided to provide egg with minimum weight of 46 gm on all school working days. Eggs with 'A' medium grade with Agmark specification are procured at state level tender by following the provisions of The Tamil Nadu Transparency in Tender Act, 1998 and Rules 2000 framed there under. During transportation of grains from state to the noon meal centre, GPS tracking is done to avoid any malpractice and similarly for quality control earmarked bag with distinct colour are being used to avert adulteration of food grains.

7.2.1 Preparedness during natural calamities

The fund and food items transfer is made 45 days in advance to make sure, no school suffers from cash shortage. These two things have been incorporated in policy guidelines but there were situations when officials have to take immediate actions and that is not in policy guidelines.For example, during rainy season there are challenges in storage, when there is lack of fully shaded godown. When asked about the benefits to the producers (farmers) during natural disaster, officials reported that they don't have very effective policy for them as such. During summer's provision for additional expenses been made for providing water tankers to the Noon Meal Centers for cooking food.

7.2.2 Public policy and institutional risks

The officials reported that, in order to ensure transparency and accountability, as per guidelines, all Noon Meal Centre have to display following updates for the community: number of children enrolled, number of children given MDM, daily menu and ration for primary and upper primary children on regular basis. Target has also been fixed for each official to conduct surprise checks at the time of serving MDM. A state level steering cum monitoring committee under the chairmanship of chief secretary to Government has been constituted by the state government. In addition District and Block level committees have been formed to review and monitor the progress of the scheme at their administrative levels. A special initiative, since 2013, of conducting Social Audit has been introduced to create awareness among the general public and to encourage committee participation. The accounts of the noon meal centre are placed before the Gram Sabha twice in a year (January 26th and August 15th), in which the students, teachers, mothers and public, participate actively and the program is discussed in details. Under management information system, the details are updated monthly to the government of India pertaining to children benefited under MDM, noon meal centers, kitchen cum store, gas connection, water facility, movement of supplies made from the TNCSC, bill raised and settled, details of cook cum helpers engaged etc. are uploaded in block and district levels.

7.2.3 Logistical and Infrastructure related risks

Joint Director (NMP) reported that, as per the norms of the central government only one post of cook cum helper is allowed for the strength of 25 beneficiaries and an honorarium of Rs 1000/ is allowed in the sharing pattern of 60:40 between centre and state. whereas the Government of Tamil Nadu, in order to provide quality, healthy, safe and delicious food for children, have appointed three staff, namely organizer (Salary Rs 7650-Rs 10,478), Cook (Rs 4380- Rs 5,055), Cook assistant (Rs 3368 -Rs 4380) in each centre. They are classified as 'Part Time Permanent Employees'. Other benefits such as: Special Monthly Pension, Lumsum payment at the time of retirement Rs 60000/- to organizer and Rs 25000/- to cook and cook assistant since February 2016, Festival Advance, Pongal Bonus, Hill and Winter Allowance, Special Provident Fund cum Gratuity scheme, Additional Charge allowance, Family Benefit Funds, New Health Insurance Scheme, General Provident Fund, Casual Leave, Maternity Leave to noon meal employees, Voluntary Retirement. The officials reported that getting trained and efficient employees are very difficult; therefore these benefits are provided to attract good talent and motivate them to work.It was mentioned in Tamil Nadu guidelines that to create 'smoke free atmosphere' under modernisation, LPG connection should be avail to all the noon meal centres. It has been provided exclusively out from the State Funds. During field visit it was observed that there are centers in Chennai and Kanchipuram who are still using wood for cooking although they have facility cylinders. The reason they reported was they kept LPG Gas as an emergency option. The gas cylinder has not been delivered, food get cooked faster on wood and they are comfortable with this practice by knowing that how harmful the fumes are for their health.

7.2.4 Political Risks

Principal Secretariat reported that in Tamil Nadu political involvement is very strong and plays important role in implementing each and every social welfare scheme before independence era. The main reason behind this is the competitive interest among political parties that help in sustaining welfare schemes very well. Secondly, it was mentioned that high literacy has helped in making such schemes successful at grassroots level. He reported that at grass root level information, communication and education in very strong, communities are not only aware but also demand of the Menu for which their children are entitled. It also came in light that currently Bureaucratic culture can be seen in implementation of the scheme. It can be more effective if community is involved in planning too. For better result strong monitoring and accountability needs to be done from both side i.e community as well as officials. PDS works in Tamil Nadu is nicely implemented. Surplus food of 15 days is available in every centre. Improved infrastructure and manpower for effective implementation is needed. Salary of manpower involved is very less that create hurdle in their motivation. State provides funds for the food grains for Std 9 & 10. Populist approach is more important than just political involvement.

The above finding shows that Tamil Nadu has been working in identifying risks and invested in efforts for managing the resources and reducing the number of errors while implementation. But still there is lot of scope to work on.

7.3 GUJARAT

The Mid-Day Meal at the state level is administered by Department of Education and Commissioner (MDM), who is supported by one Joint Commissioner and two Assistant Commissioner.

7.3.1 Public policy and institutional risk

In most of the district NGOs (Akshapatra, Sri Shakti, Nayak Foundation and Paras Agro) have been involved under Public Private Partnership (PPP) for providing meals through centralized kitchen by following MHRD Guidelines. The Deputy Collector (MDM) reported that by using this model, mechanized production has decreased contamination level in food. Since the food is prepared at central location monitoring is easy for checking meals. As per food security Act 2013, all cook cum helpers have been given training through SETCOM (BISEG). They all got training under the supervision of Principal Secretary, Commissioner of MDM, Gandhinagar, Senior Food Safety Officer, CDPO from ICDS and Deputy Collector MDM. The main content of the program was on health and cleanliness, prevention of raw material under hygienic condition, guidelines for nutrition and food safety, how to cook, financial and administrative matters, also strategy for implementation.

7.3.2 Managerial and Operational risk

For ensuring lifting of fair average quality of food grains from The Gujarat State Civil Corporation, inspection is done at district level. To protect food grain from wastage from rodents, galvanized containers are provided to MDM centre. Timely availability of Fund is ensured by either e-transfer or IFMS (Integrated Finance Management System). The state government released grants to districts in advance for smooth functioning of the scheme. In every school Mid-Day Meal roster is maintained by the local authority. During serving, parents can visit and taste the food on spot. To monitor the quality of food grains and meals, twice a year, NABL accredited lab has been assigned to test the sample for the presence of nutrients and presence of microbes as per norms under Mid-Day Meal scheme. In addition, Social Audit is been carried out by Mahatma Gandhi Labour Institute, Ahmedabad to monitor the implementation of scheme at grassroots level.

7.3.3 Logistical and infrastructure related risks

All most all the MDM centers in state are having LPG connections. Central government provides fund for construction of kitchen-cum stores to the State Government. The state government handovers this fund to the Sarva Siksha Abhiyan for the construction of kitchen cum stores. The concept of standardized model kitchen cum store has been initiated by the state in 2015-2016. The work is undertaken through Sarva Siksha Abhiyan and technical expertise is shared by Akshaya Patra. Modernization of 500 MDM kitchens was undertaken at the unit cost of 4.50 lakhs in various schools. Total 24,303 kitchens cum store have been constructed through convergence till date. The School Management committee purchase and maintained the kitchen devises Rs.5000. Serving utensils are available in each school. Government of Gujarat contributes for providing eating utensils. The utensils are also provided through community participation. To maintain the quality of food, the teachers of primary schools have been instructed to taste and take meal with school children on rotational basis.

7.3.4. Political Risks

In Gujarat though the operation is given to other NGO's, their involvement is limited. They strictly follow guidelines provided by MHRD. It seems that they are totally dependent on private bodies to fill the gap of demand and supply. Government role is limited to monitoring the status and financial transactions. Community role and responsibility in PPP mole is also reduced. For example, they can't examine the quality of ingredients NGO's use in preparation, how they prepare, their hygiene practices etc. Recently in 2017, the much –lauded initiative of Gujarat government to serve breakfast to government school kids besides mid day meals, seems to be partially successful as the scheme has been benefiting only a handful. According to the report mentioned in the DNAI, the principal of Government Gujarati Medium School in Naroda which comes in eastern Ahmedabad reported that the children in the school only get Mid-Day Meal and no breakfast. During the study it was observed that in eastern region of Ahmadabad where meals are catered by Sir Shakti Organization, the quality of meal is not up to the mark as compared to meal provided in western part of Ahmedabad, where meal is supplied by Akshayapatra Foundation. Though it was reported by senior official all NGOS followed the same Menu across the region, it was observed that Sri Shakti not following the norms and providing very simple and weekly menu is almost same. Whereas, the menu provided in Western Ahmedabad schools is much better in terms of variety and nutritional value. Same has been reported by NilamGoswami, Principal of Shela Primary School that the kids at her school don't get the breakfast. Likewise, the Gujarat government also decided to continue Mid-Day Meal even during summer vacations in schools at 51 Tehsils of Ahmedabad and some other Districts that come under drought almost every year. But due to bureaucratic approach and lack of coordination between different departments created risk for the implementation of the scheme.

Recently, an issue was highlighted in The Indian Express newspaper (2019), that the Revenue Department had issued the Drought declaration Certificate (DDC) on October 30, 2018, declaring moderate /severe drought in 51 Tehsils of Ahmedabad and other districts. The certificate stated, the declaration of drought would come into effect on 1st December 2018 and would continue to be in effect for six months from this date unless revoked earlier by an order of the state government. However, since the drought certificate "expired" on May 31 2019, office of the Commissioner, MDM Scheme, issued a circular on very same day addressing the Collector Office of those 11 drought affected districts. Accordingly, MDM scheme and Doodh Sanjeevani Yojna (under which fortified milk is provided to the children) were continued in the schools of those drought affected areas during summer vacation as per the guidelines of the Supreme Court. After completing this period, no instruction has been received from Revenue Department to extend the DDC, from June 1, 2019, and mentioned that MDM and Doodh Sanjeevani Yojna will again start once the schools open. In charge Commissioner of MDM scheme, J.D Desai said the drought notification of Revenue Department expired on May 2019, after that they have not yet extended the notification.

7.4 DISCUSSION

By analyzing both mechanisms in Tamil Nadu and Gujarat, (decentralized or centralized kitchen), Risk and Challenges exist in both circumstances. In both states, to ensure transparency and accountability of its operations, Risk Identification and mitigation is needed. There are several management studies that suggested,

Risk needs to be identified and managed by well structured systematic process. It includes all type of Risks, whether it is under control or not by the organization.

By using the Supply Chain Framework, it has been found that some of the factors may affect the supply chain of Mid-Day Meal Scheme in both the mechanisms. Though Tamil Nadu is having good internal coordination and upgrading digitally from Top to Grassroots level, still they need to work in more structured and systematic manner to identify Risk.

The study shows that the governance framework that has been used by Tamil Nadu (Decentralized model) is very much closer to the Supply Chain Framework. The most important factor that makes Tamil Nadu framework successful is the involvement/commitment and transparency among stakeholders (politicians, administrative officers & community participation). One of the important factors they shared was whenever election happened and a new political party came in power, they didn't stop the resources or reduced the budget of previous social welfare schemes. In fact they added more budgets and provided more services, resources to those particular ongoing schemes. Social welfare schemes were never hampered in any scenario. Monthly basis meeting with all the stakeholders and sharing progress report gives a value addition and keeps tab on the scheme. This is equally important factor that makes supply chain more sustainable. TN is having their own guidelines based on the baseline studies, demographic profile and resources available in the state. The high literacy has supported in making such schemes successful at grassroots level. At grassroots level information, communication and education in very strong. Communities are not only aware but also demand for the Menu children entitled. In addition, they are providing food to 9th and 10th std children and the entire expenditure is met out of state funds. TN is also providing eggs with an Agmark on all school working days. While transportation of grains from state to the noon meal centre takes place, GPS tracking is being done to avoid any type of malpractice. For quality control earmarked bag with distinct color is being used to avert adulteration of food grains. It is also mentioned that they always have 45 days buffer stock/ funds in both TNCSC and in schools in case of natural calamities like (heavy rainfall).

As per the norms of the Government of India only one post of cook cum helper is allowed for the strength of 25 beneficiaries and an honorarium of Rs 1000/ is allowed in the sharing pattern of 60:40 between centre and state. whereas the Government of Tamil Nadu, in order to provide quality, healthy, safe and delicious food for children, have appointed three staff, namely organizer (Salary Rs 7650-Rs 10,478), Cook (Rs 4380- Rs 5,055), Cook assistant (Rs 3368 -Rs 4380) The other benefits such as: Special Monthly Pension, Lumsum payment at the time of retirement, Festival Advance, Pongal Bonus, Hill and Winter Allowance, Special Provident Fund cum Gratuity scheme, Additional Charge allowance to noon meal organizers, Family Benefit Funds, New Health Insurance Scheme, General Provident Fund, Casual Leave, Maternity Leave to noon meal employees, Voluntary Retirement. The officials reported that getting trained and efficient employees is very difficult; hence these are the benefits that attract them and motivate them to work. It has also been seen that they have good coordination between other departments and schemes for better impact. This shows that they have already identified those risks in supply chain and have tried to mitigate those issues at various levels.

Now a days In India, the increased focus on internal controls in Government sector is due to the change and development taking place in the environment in which the Indian Government operates. One of the examples is Public Private Partnerships (PPPs). According to studies, there is a large gap in demand and supply of essential social and economic infrastructure and services. The Government is, therefore, actively promoting Public Private Partnerships in the key infrastructure sectors of transport, power, urban infrastructure, tourism, railways and also in many Flagship programs (such as Mid-Day Meal Scheme) for producing accelerated infrastructure investments and minimizing the infrastructure deficits in the country.

Henceforth, increased role of private sector as a partner in developmental and similar program of government raises a question on the productive use of government funds placed at the disposal of private organisations. In order to provide a fair comprehensive, as well as balanced assessment of such contract/partnerships to the Government and public, it is therefore essential to focus on identifying the Risks and systematic internal control framework in the formulation and execution of these PPPs. Government of Gujarat supply food by PPP model in most of the Urban Schools. Under the PPP model, community participation is very less, government role is only limited to monitoring the status and financial transaction and they are totally dependent on the agencies that prepare and supply meals. In this scenario, probability of Risk is very high. It is very important to control on how they are utilizing the fund, the quality and quantity of meal provided to the children. In Gujarat more than 100 contractual cook lost their job with centralized mechanism. Waste of food was found in the study where the food comes from NGOs.

Though Akshaypatra Foundation prepares food hygienically, the taste was missing. Students miss the local taste and hence waste food. On the other side in eastern part of Ahmedabad where Sri Shakti is assigned, hygiene is the big question. In fact the ingredients they used for preparation is not up to the mark. Most of the student doesn't like the meal provided and go outside the campus to eat from road side hawkers. During lunch it was observed that they were just eating unhealthy carbs like local deep fried snacks or chips. Government seems tobe only concerned about the numbers. How many children are present and how many of them had food. They don't bother about the portion of food students are eating. It was observed that 2 or 3 girls sitting together and sharing food from same plate and it looks like it was normal for teachers who are responsible for monitoring. In Gujarat, 1.45 lakh children under the age six were suffering from the worst category of malnutrition, ie Severe Acute Malnutrition (SAM) and 5.13 Lakhs School going children are suffering from malnourishment and anemia (dnai.in, 2015). Government should not only focus on only numbers but also improvement in nutrition status is needed for the development of the nation. We can't say Mid-Day Meal scheme is successful by just achieving only one objective.

There are list of studies that shows huge gap between budgeting and forecasting where the funds as per the norms are found to be inadequate. Drinking water facilities are not available, the transporters that have been entrusted with the responsibility of providing the grains to the schools were found avoid going to the interiors of the districts. Thus, the demand is not matched by the transport supplies. Hence it comes under managerial and operational risks. It was also found that the system of monitoring is being defeated by the lack of infrastructural facilities available with the Bock level officers. It was reported that no local conveyances or facilities/allowance are provided to them for the monitoring purpose and implementation of MDMS. Such issues come under logistical and infrastructure risk framework. There is a policy gap where the cooks who were entitled to get paid at the rate of Rs 0.30 paise per child day, in case, where there are only 50 or less students, the maximum wages received are only Rs 15 per day. Therefore those cooks are more interested to work in other scheme (NREGS) where they get Rs 100 per day. Risk from framework is implementing agency effectiveness, where it was found the gram panchayat who has been delegated with the responsibility of the implementation were found no or negligible interested in the process. On behalf of them, the teachers who were supposed to be in classroom and teach were busy in providing the necessary facilities for the implementation of the scheme. Risk from framework was in community involvement; as per guidelines micro-nutrients tablets were being provided to the children on a regular basis. Some tribal parents even opposed against tablets. Risk from framework was in information, education and communication where it was found that parents involvement in MDMS was very less due to lack of awareness and benefits of the scheme. In village where parents are working under some scheme they usually asked their children to sit at home and do household chores. Risk from framework was in capacity building, it was found that there is lack of availability of skilled data entry operators and dedicated management information system (MIS) cell at district level.

Incomplete information was provided by the school is also a major issue reported by the officers. Once we indentify the list of the Risks in supply chain, it is important to prioritize the Risks. For example probability of occurrence of the Risks, consequences of the Risks and cost and resources required for the mitigation of the Risks. Government institutions are large organisations, managing huge resources tend to have larger exposure to Risk. Therefore, the need of identifying Risk and the process of controlling is necessary to ensure transparency and accountability of its operations.

CHAPTER VIII

AWARENESS OF MID DAY MEAL SCHEME AMONG BENEFICIARIES AND INDICATOR FOR ASSESMENT

In the previous chapter we discussed about the origin, and Supply Chain of the MDMS. The present chapter deals with the field experiences in Tamil Nadu and Gujarat which includes existing perceptions and observations regarding the scheme. On the basis of supply chain management principles, the researcher presented some indicators for assessment of the process.

To improve the supply chain process of any scheme, time to time perceptions and suggestions are required. During the survey in both the state, students/teachers/parents/cooks were inquired about their perceptions and if any suggestions they want to share regarding MDMS. In first stage, selection was done of two districts then after from each district two blocks were selected possessively from both the states. Two schools from each block were selected randomly. Overall, 16 government /government aided schools was selected from both the states. In next stage from each school, 8 principals, 5 teachers and 10 students were randomly selected for the study. In Gujarat, centralized kitchen system was observed, and while in Tamil Nadu, the decentralized kitchen practices were observed. Total 160 students, 80 teachers, 16 principals across 16 schools from both the states were interviewed during the data collection process.

8.1 CHILDREN PERSPECTIVE REGARDING MDMS

In Tamil Nadu, almost all students reported that they eat MDM at school premises only and they don't participate in cooking. They shared that they stand in a row, wash their hand and plates and then sit together. None of the children reported objection from their parents for in-taking meal at school. In fact many parents insisted there children to eat only meal which is prepared in school premises. All the selected schools were having drinking water facilities in school itself. When asked about their suggestions regarding Menu, the students reported that till date their views regarding menu has not been captured by anybody, but they are willing to participate in the process of preparing Menu.

In Gujarat, 50 % of the students reported that they had meals in schools only, 35 % don't eat MDM in schools; and few of them reported that they bring food from home and while few eat outside campus. It was been observed that these students belonged to schools where Sri Shakti Foundation was delivering the meals. More than 50% of students sat together during eating whereas 21% students reported that they sometimes sit together but not regularly. These are mostly those who either bring food from home or they eat outside. When asked about their parents whether they object to eat MDM, 84 % student reported that there is no objection, but 17 % said yes their parents ask not to eat MDM. All schools were having drinking water facilities.

Students were asked whether they bring plates from home, 13 percent reported "yes". They brought either Tiffin or polybag to collect meal from home. During further probing, when asked from head master of that school about the issue, he accepted and mentioned that they have very limited plates that too have been sponsored by the community.

Table 16: Students responses regarding MDMS

Questions	Tamil Nadu				Gujarat			
	Yes	No	Sometimes	N	Yes	No	Sometimes	N
Do you eat MDM at school premises?	80	0	0	80	40	28	12	80
Do you participate in cooking?	0	80	0	80	Not Applicable			
Do you sit together while eating MDM?	80	0	0	80	63		17	80
Do your parents asked not to eat MDM in the school?	0	80	0	80	0	67	13	80
Do you have drinking facilities in school?	80	0	0	80	80	0	0	80
Do you bring plates from home?	0	80	0	80	10	70	0	80
Did someone asked about the choice of food you want to eat?	0	80	0	80	0	62	18	80
Do you think that student should involve in preparing menu?	80	0	0	80	80	0	0	80

8.2 PARENT'S RESPONSE REGARDING MDMS

Out of the total 48 respondents from parent's category, majority of the respondents, nearly 87 % did not have a regular employment either in the government or private sector. They were mostly self-employed in small business or in agriculture. Almost all parents reported that their children receive adequate meals in school in both the states. In Gujarat, few parents reported that there are few children who bring food from home. In both the states, Parents were further asked whether they are aware of any guidelines under MDMS. Almost all parents in Gujarat (where food is prepared through centralized kitchen mechanism) were unaware about the prescribed MDMS guidelines. The only thing they knew that their children is getting meal. They were not having information regarding what their children are receiving, why and how they are receiving, and parent's role in monitoring and about receiving meal is their child right. On the other hand, in Tamil Nadu, most of the parents were aware about the menu, especially mentioned that their children are getting eggs on daily basis. They also said that they can visit anytime school for monitoring while cooking and distribution of meals.

All parents from both the states were happy with the scheme as their children were provided daily meals and do not go hungry. They felt that due to MDMS they don't have any worry for their children food and education. None of the parents made any complaint that their children developed any kind of health problems after eating MDM. Moreover; some parents felt that they have seen some improvement in their child development. All parents agreed that, MDM has encouraged them to send their children to school, thereby reducing the dropout rate and simultaneously reducing the child labor in the area. Many parents even expressed that because of MDM, they are sending their girls to school instead asking them to do household work. In Tamil Nadu, more number of parents is aware as compared to Gujarat, about the Parent-Teacher Association (PTA), which discussed about MDM implementation during meeting and about its monitor.

Table 17. Parents response regarding MDMS

Questions	Tamil Nadu			Gujarat		
	Yes	No	N	Yes	No	N
Children eats MDM at school premises	24		24	20	4	24
Reasons for not eating MDM						
No taste					1	n=4
children not liking it					3	
Awareness among parents regarding government standard for MDMS						
Entitlement of food norms	24		24		24	24
Display of weekly menu	24			4	20	
Toll free number	17	7			24	
Food security Allowance	24				24	
Government standards practice in school						
Display of weekly menu	24		24	3	21	24
Toll free number	17	7			24	
Food security Allowance	24				24	
School committees involvement in functioning MDM						
committees involved in the designing of the program	24		24		24	24
committee (SMC/PTA) manage and monitor the MDM	24				24	
Community participation in MDM						
Helping in cooking food		24	24		24	24
Monitoring	24				24	
Involvement in planning and implementation	18	6			24	
Mobilizing and motivating other parents to send their children to school	24				24	
Benefits of MDMS						
Nutritional development	24		24	20	4	24
Child is studying	24			17	6	
Decrease drop outs	24			20	4	
Child is not hungry	24			20	4	
Child is getting regular food	24			20	4	

8.3 TEACHERS RESPONSES REGARDING MDMS

The third category of stakeholders was the school head master and the teacher numbering total 48 (1 headmaster and 2 teachers from 16 schools from both the states). Teachers were interviewed so as to obtain the information regarding the quality of food provided, the official co-operation they receive, problems they faced during the implementation and its impact on overall teaching. Regarding the Menu for MDM, in both state teachers reported that they do not having any deciding role; it comes from district officials. Menu is usually decided between district officials and the agency involved in delivering food. For example, in Tamil Nadu Noon Meal Program Centre and in Gujarat NGOs are involved in the finalizing menu. In Tamil Nadu, teachers further revealed that, however, at the school level it is either the headmaster or the Parent Teacher Association (PTA), decides on the selection of vegetables that are available to be provided to the children. Where as in Gujarat, the headmaster and teacher responsibility is limited to testing and supervising the process of meal distribution among children. During observation and also while discussing about the issues, it was felt that in Gujarat, teachers were free from most of the responsibilities as compared to their counterparts in Tamil Nadu. In Gujarat, teachers were bothered about the monitoring format that needs to be filled on daily basis. In most of the schools during the survey in Gujarat, it was observed that, though it is mandatory for headmaster and teachers to check and taste the food, none of the them did their job seriously. They were not in practice of monitoring students whether they are eating or wasting food in dustbin. In one school of Ahmedabad, where food was delivered by Sri Shakti NGO, most of the students either brought food from home or ate outside school premises and teachers were comfortable with this act. Very casual approach has been noticed by most of the teachers in Gujarat who are involved under MDM. whereas in Tamil Nadu, the teachers and headmaster who are in charge for supervision, they seriously followed the guidelines, fully documented each and every activity they are supposed to perform under MDMS. This showed their sincerity and commitment towards their assigned job.

At the school level, the monitoring of MDM was carried out by different groups like Gram Panchayat, PTA, MTA, etc. In Tamil Nadu, PTA and MTA including teachers were highly active in monitoring and supervision. During the study it was observed that every day one or other group was available during preparation of meal and recess time to monitor the distribution of meal and also to monitor whether children are in discipline or not. They have a practice of asking student whether they are liking food or not, their choice of food etc.

Whereas in Gujarat, teachers were occupied in monitoring activity by filling the assigned format on daily basis. Parents Teachers Association involvement was negligible. None of the teachers felt that MDM in any way disrupts teaching in both the states. Teachers agreed that there is increase in enrolment and decrease in dropout rate due to the scheme in both the states. Majority of teachers acknowledged that, the level of interest among the children towards studies have increased due to MDM. All the respondents felt that MDM is a noble initiative under which children receive nutritious meal. They also shared that there was no opposition from anybody/ association towards MDM and majority of teachers responded that they get timely co-operation from the officials regarding the program implementation.

Table 18: Teacher responses regarding MDMS

Questions	Tamil Nadu			Gujarat		
	Yes	No	N	Yes	No	N
Budget sufficient to cover all expenses	24		24	24		24
Involvement in preparation of weekly Menu		24	24		24	24
Base line and impact evaluations carried out, or are any planned	24		24		24	24
Has the program's actual cost per child per year been calculated	24		24	24		24
Aware of the government standard regarding						
Entitlement of food norms	24		24	24		24
Display of weekly menu	24		24	24		24
Toll free number	24		24		24	24
Food security Allowance	24		24	24		24
Food Safety	24		24	24		24

Questions	Tamil Nadu			Gujarat		
Practice in school						
Display of weekly menu	24		24	24		24
Toll free number		24	24		24	24
Food security Allowance	24		24	20	4	24
Analysis of food requirements and supply options		24				24
food quality norms and food quality control mechanisms	24		24		24	24
school committees that involves parents, teachers, and local community in the implementation of MDMs	24		24		24	24
Community participation in MDM programs	24		24		24	24
Any mechanisms that are in place to systematically address issues of stigmatization in school	24		24		24	24
Any support groups in place at the school level or community level to respond to specific stigma issues faced by teachers, cook and students?	24				24	
National school curriculum cover any health, hygiene, nutrition and life skill	24			24		
There pre- and in-service training provided to teachers to teach this (any health, hygiene, nutrition and life skill) curriculum?	24		24	24		24
health-related knowledge covered in this curriculum integrated into school examinations	24		24	24		24
Do you feel that the MDM disrupts teaching anyway		24	24		24	
proper co-operation from the officials as well as the parents regarding MDM in school	24		24		24	

8.4 COOK RESPONSE REGARDING MDMS

The last category of respondents was cooks and other MDMS organizers. A total of 16 respondents were interviews as they are directly involved in all activities of the scheme at school. All 8 selected schools in Tamil Nadu were having kitchen and store in school premises only. Though LPG gas was allotted to all the schools, still firewood for cooking was in practice in few schools. The cook followed the instruction of headmaster regarding menu for the day. In all the cases, the cooks were having one helper and one MDM organizer to oversee and maintain all the records related to MDMS. All cooks and helpers were highly satisfied by the Tamil Nadu Government for taking multiple initiatives for social security. Almost all cooks believe that feeding children is like feeding God. With that mindset if we do our work, productivity will automatically be high and it will give positive results. Finally, all the cooks and organizers interviewed felt that MDM must continue as it gives the children a definite meal per day which they feel is very important for holistic development of the children.

After recording observation at different levels and discussion with different set of stakeholders under the scheme, it reflects that if the existing discrepancies in supply chain will exist, the quality of meal provided to our beneficiaries will never be as expected and therefore it will be difficult to achieve all objectives of the scheme. By achieving the enrollment rate doesn't make the scheme successful. A Childs physical, mental and psychological health is equally important.

CHAPTER IX

CONCLUSION AND RECOMMENDATION

CONCLUSION & RECOMMENDATION

Background

The issues related to quality of food grains, quantity and its distribution at school may not always lieas the responsibility at the school level, if seen through the broader perspective of involvement and performance between various actors throughout the supply chain. Agarwal.O.P, Somnathan.T.V. (2005), insisted on quality of policy making within a broad sector rather than on issues of strategic choice between sectors. Author also suggested doing valid disagreements/debates prior to the policy making on to what is the right policy in a given sector, in a given situation can giver better roadmap for execution. As we have discussed earlier that MDMS is a complex intervention, hence Supply Chain Management is a key factor in program delivery and managing performance for such kind of intervention. The same has insisted by Edward A. (2002), that public policy should be customer focused and ensure successful public/private partnerships, performance outcomes that are customer driven, planning and policy oversight that is performance based.

MDMS includes activities and interactions among different stakeholders at different levels for effective implementation. Hence probability of negligence can easily occur. Till date, this scheme is been run based on the reports that pointed operational issues and patchworks activities/solution were performed for their resolution. Very few research works have focused on the "WHY" aspect of it.(Ranjita Sabkota in (2015),R,Kadari and S.M Roy (2016), Priyanka Singh,.etal., (2018), Roy, Vivek., et al.(2017).

For the current study, the researcher selected two different states belonging to different geography and demography (Tamil Nadu & Gujarat). These are the two states where MDMS was implemented back before country independence. Currently, Tamil Nadu is delivering meals through decentralized process in all the districts, whereas Gujarat switched to Centralized kitchen process by involving NGOs covering majority of districts.

There are many states that are following the implementation model of Tamil Nadu. Therefore the key interest behind the research work was to explore the existing model, know about flawless implementation with minimal cases of incidences, types of stakeholders involved, their coordination and interaction, management of supply chain and recent techniques they are using for monitoring and evaluation of the program. The main purpose of conducting this study was to understand Mid Day Meal operations from Supply Chain perspective. As per the supply chain practice, the performance of any project or scheme depends on critical factors related to its supply chain configuration which is linked with the program objectives. These critical factors can be within and outside of the control of the program. Therefore the objective of the study was to identify internal and external factors influencing supply chain process in terms of policy framework, financial capacity, institutional capacity & coordination, management & accountability structures, design & implementation, role of community, psycho social school environment, and identify waste and non value adding elements within different processes. By using SCM tools &technique, *the study first addressed*:

The stakeholder's involvement in MDMS. A mapping exercise was done which helped in identifying their requirement and managing their expectation during the process. The study analyzed all activities/actions that are carried out from national to block level through the SCM perspective. The activities were procurement, transportation & distribution, Warehousing/Storage, processing, preparation of meals, physical resources and quality control. The study identified risk and challenges that has been traditionally defined as possibilities related to danger, loss, injury or other consequences. By identifying the risks and challenges it helped in understanding the conceptualization and implementation of the scheme. Perception and suggestions from the beneficiaries' point of view were covered along with some indicators that can be used for the assessment.In addition, the study also elaborates the transformation in the scheme which took place during the duration in past twenty years. It tries to explain, why the situation demands for a policy, how it is being implemented, a need to keep on modifying the processes and also introduction of new mechanism/factors for effective execution.

1. Importance of Stakeholders Mapping

The study identified internal and external stakeholders through mapping exercise in Mid-day meal Scheme. Mapping helped in identifying various stakeholders at different execution levels as per the established process for their requirement and managing their expectation. Mid-day meal scheme is a government driven program therefore active involvement of internal stakeholders can been seen i.e. government institutions at various levels, however external stakeholders have equally important role in the supply chain for making the program successful and sustainable. The role of the farmer in MDMS has deep impacts. They are the strong pillar of the scheme by supplying grains in subsidize rate to the centre. The study indicates towards the governance framework which has been used by Tamil Nadu (Decentralized kitchen model) is very much closer to tools developed by The World Bank on supply chain based on Lean principles. The important factor that makes Tamil Nadu framework successful is the involvement/commitment and transparency among critical stakeholders (politicians, administrative officers & community participation). One of the important observations which were shared was whenever election happened and a new political party came in power, they didn't stop the resources or reduced the budget of previous social welfare schemes. In fact they added more budgets and provided more services, resources to those particular ongoing schemes. Social welfare schemes were never hampered in any scenario. The same governance framework was highlighted by Carolyn J.Hill, Laurance E. Lynn Jr. (2005), where author insisted in shifting from hierarchical government toward greater reliance on horizontal, hybridized and associational forms of governance for better outcome.

Amartya Sen, Noble Prize Winning Economist has observed that in India, hunger is not enough of a political priority. The public expenditure on health is very low and funds allocated to programs like child nutrition remains unspent. It is only in States like Tamil Nadu that he sees a political will and commitment to tackle these issues by setting goals like achieving the status of a "malnutrition free State".

Frequent monitoring and discussion on the status with Principal Secretariat and among all the stakeholders on 23rd of every month is an important activity/factor to keep check on the scheme. In Tamil Nadu, media is also playing an important role/factor as external stakeholders. In every four months, Principal Secretary share recent development of the program and also want feedbacks regarding further improvement with the community via radio or email.TN is having their own guidelines based on the baseline studies, demographic profile and resources available in the state. The high literacy rate in state has supported in making the scheme successful at grassroot level. It was found that at grassroots level information, communication and education among stakeholders is very strong. Communities are aware about the entitlements and demand constant information on menu for which their children are entitled. This type of involvement of external and internal stakeholders gives strong and sustainable base to the system for better outcome. The same has been discussed by B. Gail Smith. (2008), who insisted that interpersonal trust and working to standards are both important to build more sustained local and many conserved food supply chains. Further suggested that cooperation among food manufacturers, retailers, NGOs, government and farmer organizations is vital in order to raise standards for supply chains and to enable farmers to adopt more sustainable agriculture practices.

2. Need of Risk Identification and Mitigation

By analyzing both mechanisms in Tamil Nadu and Gujarat, (decentralized or centralized kitchen), it was observed that Risk and Challenges exist in both mechanisms. In both states, to ensure transparency and accountability of its operations, risk identification and mitigation is needed. It includes all type of risks, whether internal or external.

To control the risk of malpractices, TN has been following various practices like providing eggs with an Agmark on all school working days. Introduction of GPS tracking system of grains from state to the noon meal centre takes place during transportation. For quality control year marked bags with distinct color are being used to avert adulteration of food grains. It was also observed that a buffer stocks and fund of 45 days was maintained at both TNCSC and in schools to manage any incidents related to natural calamities like (heavy rainfall).

In state of Gujarat, it was found during the study that parent's involvement in MDMS was very less due to lack of awareness about the benefits of the scheme. In rural areas, parents are working in fields and they usually asked their children to sit at home and perform household chores. It was also observed that there is lack of availability of skilled data entry operators and dedicated management information system (MIS) cell at district level. Incomplete information sharing by schools was a major issue reported by the officers.

Once we indentify the list of the risks in supply chain, it is important to prioritize the risks. For example, probability of occurrence of the risks, consequences of the risks and cost and resources required for the mitigation of the risks. Government institutions are large organisations, managing huge resources tend to have larger exposure to risk. Therefore, the need of identifying risk and the process of controlling is necessary to ensure transparency and accountability of its operations.

3. Increase Remuneration and Other Incentives

As per the norms of the central government only one post of cook cum helper is allowed for the strength of 25 beneficiaries and an honorarium of Rs 1000/ is allowed in the sharing pattern of 60:40 between centre and state. But in Tamil Nadu, in order to provide quality, healthy, safe and delicious food for children, three staff have been appointed, namely organizer (Salary Rs 7650-Rs 10,478), Cook (Rs 4380- Rs 5,055), Cook assistant (Rs 3368 -Rs 4380). The other benefits which are provided are such as: Special Monthly Pension, Lumsum payment at the time of retirement, Festival Advance, Pongal Bonus, Hill and Winter Allowance, Special Provident Fund cum Gratuity scheme, Additional Charge allowance to noon meal organizers, Family Benefit Funds, New Health Insurance Scheme, General Provident Fund, Casual Leave, Maternity Leave to noon meal employees, Voluntary Retirement.

The officials reported that getting trained and efficient employees is very difficult; hence the above mentioned benefits are being offered to attract and motivate employees to work. It was observed in Tamil Nadu that better coordination among departments and across schemes was happening for creating better impact. This shows that they have already identified those risks in supply chain and have tried to mitigate those issues at various levels.

4. Regular Assessment of Public Private Partnerships (PPPs)

In India, the increased focus on internal controls in government sector is due to the change and development taking place in the environment in which the Indian Government operates. One of the examples is Public Private Partnerships (PPPs). Several studies have reported that there is a large gap in demand and supply of essential social and economic infrastructure and services. The government is actively promoting Public Private Partnerships in the key infrastructure sectors of transport, power, urban infrastructure, tourism, railways and also in many Flagship programs (such as Mid-Day Meal Scheme) for producing accelerated infrastructure investments and minimizing the infrastructure deficits in the country. Henceforth, increased role of private sector as a partner in developmental and similar programs of government raises a question on the productive use of government funds placed at the disposal of private organizations. In order to provide a fair comprehensive, as well as balanced assessment of such contract/partnerships to the government and public, it is essential to focus on identifying the risks and systematic internal control framework in the formulation and execution of these PPPs.

Government of Gujarat supplies meals by PPPs model in most of the Urban Schools. Under the PPPs model, community participation is very less, government role is only limited to monitoring the status of financial transaction and state is totally dependent on the agencies that prepare and supply meals, in this scenario, probability of risk is very high. It is important to control the utilization of funds, the quality and quantity of meal provided to the children. In Gujarat more than 100 contractual cook lost their job due to implementation of centralized mechanism. Wastage of meals was found in schools in Gujarat. Though,Akshaypatra Foundation prepares hygienic meal, the taste was missing as reported by students. Students complained of missing the local taste and hence waste dmeal. In eastern part of Ahmedabad where Sri Shakti organization is assigned for meal services, hygiene was a major concern reported.It was reported that the ingredients used for preparation of meals were not of good quality. Most of the student didn't eat meals and visited outside the campus to eat from road side hawkers. During lunch either they eat local snacks or chips. It was felt that Gujarat government is only concerned about the number of meals served and stats like how many children are present, how many of them eat meals. Government was not monitoring the portion of meals students are consuming. In one of the selected sample school 2 - 3 girls were sitting together and sharing food from common plate which appeared as a common practice their for teachers.

In Gujarat, 1.45 lakh children under the age six were suffering from the worst category of malnutrition, i.e. Severe Acute Malnutrition (SAM) and 5.13 Lakhs School going children are suffering from malnourishment and anemia (dnai.in, 2015). There is health related risk that needs to be mitigated. Not only numbers of stats but improvement in nutrition status is required for the development of the nation. We can't say Mid-Day Meal scheme is successful by just achieving only one objective.

5. Awareness Level should be same among all the Stakeholders

Program effectiveness is bound to increase if similar level of understanding can be established among all the stakeholders whether internal or external. When there is a demand, required supply is provided. For e.g. in Tamil Nadu, parents knew that their children will get eggs on daily basis under the provisions of the scheme; hence they made sure during supervision that children are receiving it with meals. For promoting awareness among community and increasing its participation the state government should organized Awareness Generation Mela/ events at different levels.

6. Community Participation through Capacity Building Training Program

This study strongly recommends that community participation is vital to ensure schemes success. There are many issues that can be easily rectified at local level by involving community such as replacement of vessels, sitting mat and safe drinking water, healthcare of children, maintenance of hygienic environment in the school premises, supply of food on social occasion, community kitchen etc. Just like centralized kitchen in urban area, community kitchen can be innovated in rural areas.

Parents/ local groups can be trained and be engaged in activities like procuring, preparing, serving food to the children, monitoring of activities by their own developed roster. This accountability among community itself can give amazing result for sure. It will not only be helpful for the betterment of the scheme but also contribute in improving the overall socio economic dynamics of the local community. The same has been supported by S. Fernandez (2003),that political support from the public and the levels of task complexity both have a significant effect on organizational performance. Support from the public is positively correlated with performance, while higher complexity serves to weaken performance.

7. Introduction of Solar Cooking System

To save further degradation of forest or vegetation and control pollution, all Mid-day Meal schools should be connected with solar electricity systems as an alternative to LPG gas. It will be an eco friendly and sustainable solution for future.

8. Women Empowerment

The scheme should increase higher participation of women belonging to self help groups who are efficient in managing records and accounts. For achieving it, women who have obtained primary or upper primary education should be given preference. Such women are available within the village or in nearby adjoining villages.

9. Transportation

The essential commodities such as edible oil, condiments, salt, gas etc should be supplied along with food grains to the schools directly like implemented in state of Tamil Nadu. The process saves transportation cost, manpower and time.

10. Introduction of Home- Grown School Feeding (HFSF)

This concept focuses on produce and purchase of food grains for the Mid-day Meal program from local small scale farmers. From WFP's perspective, an HGSF program aims to both increase children's well-being and promote local agricultural production by providing an ongoing market for small landholders. The United Nations in year 2005 during World Summit recommended 'the expansion of local school feeding programs, using home-grown foods where possible' "as one of the quick impact initiative" to achieve the Millennium Development Goals, especially for rural areas facing the dual challenge of high chronic malnutrition and low agricultural productivity (World Summit Outcome, 2005; UN Millennium Project 2005a). This concept can be a value addition in MDM supply chain in India. Local cereals could be procured and stored in godowns. In case of famine like calamity occurs, such compulsion need to be exempted and flexibility should be given for supply of non-local food grains. In other words, to promote local economy, involving local farmers in the process of procurement is needed. District should be a locale for all tasks, whether it is related to procurement or distribution. This will help in using the excess quantity of grains and other ingredients at local level. Procurement at local level will have multidimensional impact as on one side fresh grains with good quality will be available and on other side this will help in reducing the length of supply chain of food grains and also it reduce the time that consume in processing at different stages among stakeholders. On the other hand it could be the motivational factors for the farmers at the local level. This will not only help in improvement in their standard of living but also this will ensure improvement of health and educational status of children. Thus the priority to local farmers is a value addition in the supply chain that will help in reducing the use of resources in terms of cost, human resources, time.

11. Focus on Quantity, Quality and Time

1. Packaging

During field visit to Tamil Nadu,it was observed that superior quality (BOPP) of packaging material is being used for preserving the grains to maintain the quality of grains throughout the season and also there are less chances of leakage either during transportation or storage. BOPP bags are better than gunny bags, they are superior in strength, are moisture resistance and rodents can't easily damage the grains which reduces probability of leakage.

2. Uses of Technology

By using technology and techniques at different levels, Tamil Nadu has controlled malpractices up to some extent. It assure the quality as well as quantity of grains from first to last level. For example, using of weighing machine during loading and unloading at school level, use of GPS tracker, use of stamp on bags as well as on eggs etc.

3. Storage

It is very important to disinfect the room/ place where grains are kept. It should be spacious with proper ventilation and lighting in the room. In past it was seen that rodents as well as pests create problems and hampered the quality of grains. Henceforth regular cleaning and pest control should be done in regular interval.

4. Storing period of grains in go-down

It is very important to analyse the period of storing grains in go-down. The maximum time duration where food grains are kept during overall supply chain is in go-down, which may affect the quality of grains. It is very important to assure how the grain has been kept at what condition.

5. Monitoring and Supervision

It should be done digitally at all levels as it will reduce time, cost and manpower. During study it was observed that at all level documentation was consuming too much time. Keeping records was a big challenge. Officials who visited schools and fill the assigned formats reported that they don't have time to enter the data again in computer. It consumes their working time.

6. Cooking and Serving Mechanism

Training of cooks on food safety and on techniques of cooking to keep nutrition intact is an important activity. Precautionary action needs to be taken while preparation by using fresh water, air tight container should be used for storage of grains. Plastic container or spoon should be avoided.

7. Time taken for preparation of food

To maintained the nutrition value it is very important to study the time taken for preparation of food and also the time taken to reach the beneficiaries. In case of centralized kitchen, meals are cooked in the early hour of the day, till the time it get served, it doesn't remain enough warm as a result children were observed wasting food is one of the key observation.

8. Ingredients used in preparation

It has been noticed that states are mostly using palm oil for cooking. There are studies that explain about the harms of palm oil. The only reason for use of palm oil could be its cost effectiveness compared to other oils. The salt and other spices should be of Agmark certification. Agmark is a certified mark employed on agricultural products in India, assuring that they confirm to a set of standards approved by the Directorate of marketing and inspection office of the Department of Agriculture.

9. Hygiene practices

The cleanliness must be maintained throughout the entire supply chain/activities at go-down, school storage, kitchen, while cooking and also among children. Not only that, drinking facilities, area where children sit and eat, the person who served food (whether they are following hygiene practices by using caps and gloves etc) need to be assure.

10. Waste of food by children

Teacher and parents who supervise should notice whether children are consuming sufficient quantity of meal or not. If children are wasting meals, they should be asked about the reason behind the act. It was noticed in Gujarat, where centralized mechanism is working successfully, wastage of meals by children is very common. Children revealed that though they are getting different variety of meal every day, the taste is missing.

11. Information Flow

As soon as orders are placed for food grains the time taken towards its release determines the overall time it will take to reach at different destinations in the entire supply chain. This could also be applied in releasing fund. As soon as the fund get released, processing start to allocate grains and forward the same for the next level. In both the situation time is crucial.

12. Transparency in selection of third party

The contract for selection of third party should mention each and every protocol that needs to be followed. The contractor selection should be based on their previous performance and preferably belonging to the local demographic region.

13. Coordination of all the activities

This is the one of the most important element of any supply chain. For the effective delivery of services, the process of reporting, storage, fund transformation, flow of information, uses of techniques and coordination among all the actors should be synced at program implementation level.

By reviewing different management studies and evaluation reports on MDMS, the researcher tried to find out some performance related indicators focusing on quality, quantity and time. All this information could be collected digitally and eventually shared with all the stakeholders from top to bottom. This will give clearer picture about the process.

12. Key Performance Indicators

Taking in account all the aspects through SCM technique, key performance indicators has been developed which can be used digitally for monitoring. The information could be shared with all the stakeholders involved, to achieve same understanding of all the activities. It is important to realize the significance of each and every activity performed in the chain to identify the trade-offs and propose new value added components.The same has been highlighted by S. Fernandez (2003),time spent managing internally seems to contribute less to performance then time spent managing the external environment. It's a high time, rather criticizing any scheme or government we need to take corrective measures to identify unwanted process and stakeholders involved and make best use of resources available.

Table 20: Performance Based Indicators

QUANTITY EFFECTIVENESS MEASURES			
Total Quantity of grains in FCI	**Quantity measures in transport**	**Go down Occupancy**	**Food serving to child**
% of Quantity Demands	Quantity lifted from FCI	Space required	Per child requirement
% of Quantity Supply	Quantity received at school	Capacity	Per child in take
% Surplus/ Shortage	Quantity lost	Space shortage	food left- unused
Grain availability at School			Food wasted by the children
Monthly requirement			
Received quantity			
% shortage			
Quality effectiveness measures			
Quality of food grains	**Quality of Packaging**	**Action taken for quality control measures**	**Quality measures during preparation**
Quality of grains delivered	Using POP bags	Pest & rodents control	Quality of ingredient used for preparation
Quality of grains received	Using gunny bags		Water quality
Time Management			
Maximum and minimum Time utilizing for floating contract/selecting contractors	Maximum and minimum Time utilizing by supplier	Maximum and minimum Time utilized in transportation	Maximum and minimum Time grains kept in godown
Maximum and minimum Time for releasing funds	Maximum and minimum Time utilizing for cooking	Maximum and minimum Time for delivering food to the schools	Maximum and minimum Time for serving food to the children

13. Recommendation for Digitalisation

Every step involved in supply chain need to be analysed for maximum utilization of available resources for sustaining the program. Currently the traditional practice of analyzing the scheme is not at all sufficient. There is huge scope for further studies on the same issues as very limited research work is available. The current study will help to construct a basic understanding of scheme through Supply Chain Management perspective and its significance.

Digital Platform (Web and Mobile Application Based) For Facilitating MDMS

The study is proposing a digital framework in Mid-day Meal Scheme through designing and implementing Electronic Mid-day Meal Network (eMDMN), an innovation that will bring together technology, people and processes to strengthen the mid-day meal supply chain by digitizing information on at all levels.

Figure 20: The Three integral parts of eMDMN

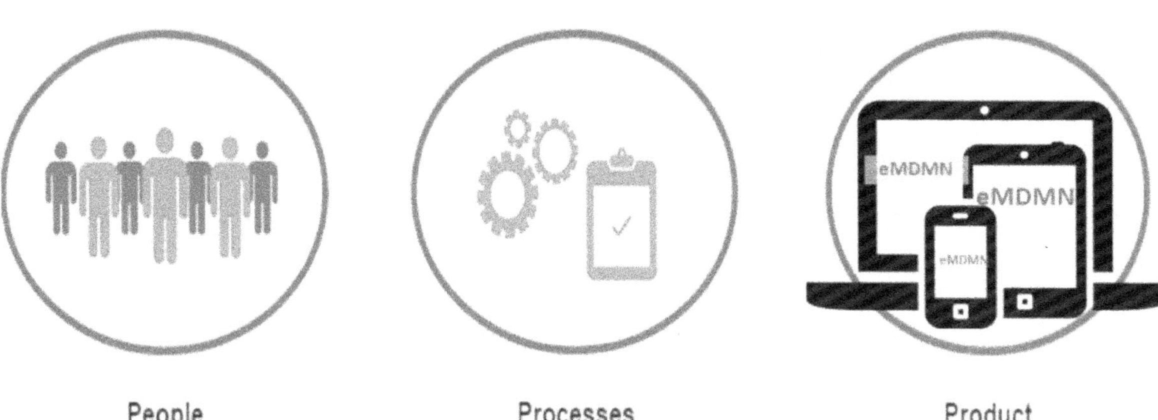

What is eMDMN?

An electronic supply chain management information system (eSCMIS) that will use Web interface/Smartphone, and IoT device with cloud-based technology to capture real-time data across the entire supply chain, from the FCI godown to the last-mile school.

Its aim will be to streamline and regularize the food grains flow network by ensuring data-driven and efficient management of the supply chain. eMDMN will help in capturing data at all levels of supply chain digitally. A mobile application can be used by all internal stake holders who are directly implementing the scheme e.g. officials of district and block level, Head master, teachers, parents, cooks etc. For external and indirect persons involved in implementation, web based interface will be helpful e.g. District collector, Food commissioner, agencies like FCI, transporters etc. Facilitating real-time monitoring of flow of goods and services through mobile based digital application and web interface will be an advantage for the scheme. Once the technology is ready a pilot can be done in some parts of country with selecting different geographic and demographic location. Later working on building capacity of all government and private personnel for supply chain management on (eMDMN) will be required for its nationwide implementation.

Figure 21: Expected change in systems strengthening and service delivery through digital intervention

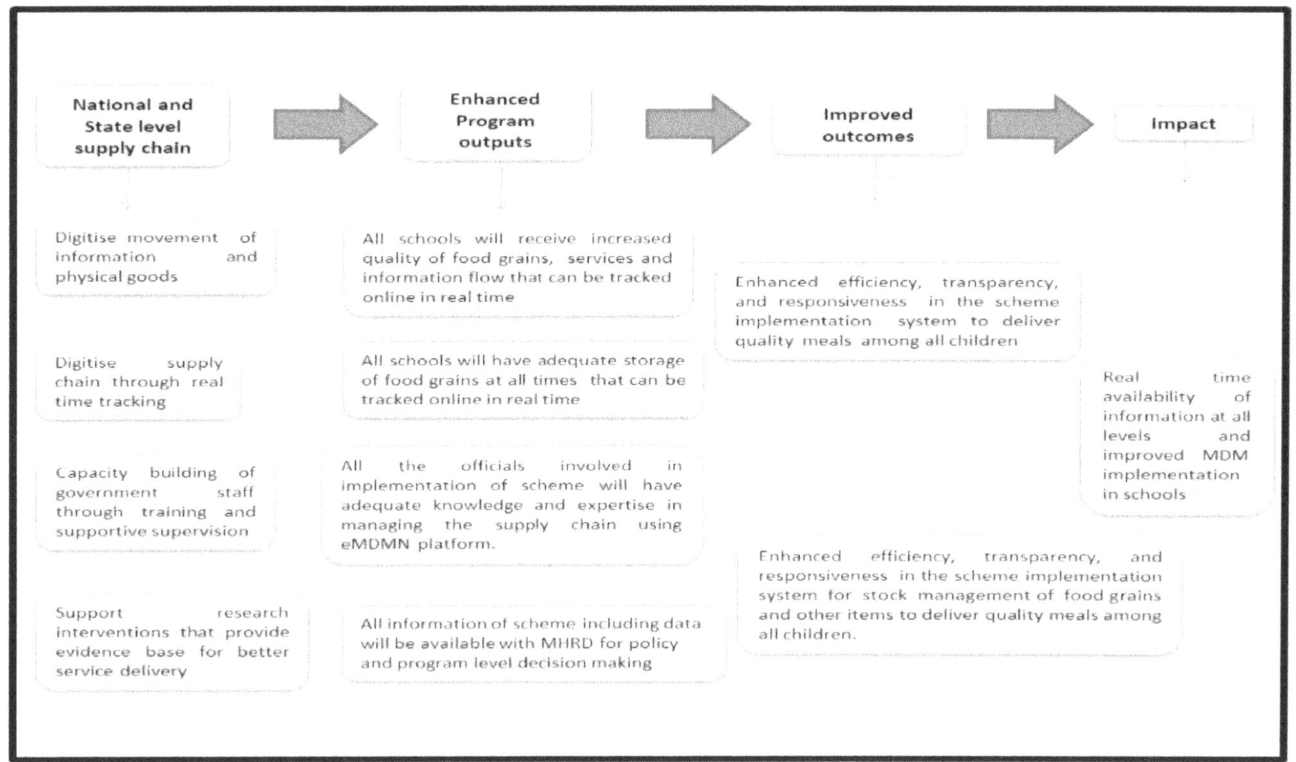

The integrated solution to supply chain management combining the use of a new technology with capacity-building can be used to strengthen governance and human resources for management at all levels of the chain. The technological component of (eMDMN)will include an easy-to-use mobile phone application that will allow all stake holders to report data on flow of food grains &related items, likestocks, consumption and movement.

This data will be stored in cloud server that will provide web-based dashboards and data analytics for project implementation officials, program managers, and policymakers to view the information in real time. The end-to-end visibility of key supply chain data will allow stakeholders to effectively manage and make decisions on operations to ensure that food grains reach to children. Tracking of transportation of food grains form FCI to school level can be monitored with help of IoT device. The IoT device will be installed on each of the vehicles transporting food grains. It will provide real time information on movement of food grains to officials involved in implementation of scheme from State to school level.

Other benefits from the digital system have been mentioned below:

- Reduction in instances of food grain stock-outs and ensured improved availability of adequate and quality meals to all targeted children.

- Reduction in utilization of food grains & related items in pre-**eMDMN** period to post-**eMDMN** period across states, on account of wastage and mismanagement, which will result into savings.

- Increase in availability rate of all important items at all schools.

Perceived Benefits

eMDMNwill standardized record-keeping practices, build state-of-the-art technology, and a strong network of trained personnel to address widespread inequities in meals coverage and it will support the state governments in overcoming constraints of infrastructure, monitoring and management information systems and human resources, often resulting in overstocking and stock-outs of grains & itemsin schools. eMDMN will create a big data architecture that will generate actionable analytics across major indicators encouraging data-driven decision making, accountability and a positive behavioral change in the mid-day system. (Figure 14).

Figure 22: Expected benefits from eMDMN

Improved stock availability	Real time Data visibility	Tools and reports	Strengthened implementation system	Replicable model
Through better visibility and standardized procedure	At all schools along with real time quality monitoring	Reports to facilitate in decision making of supply chain management	Through human resource, capacity building and leveraging technology	For state/ nation wide scale up

The program officials can view the entire supply chain from national to last mile level. They will be able to track the movement of goods and information on real time basis. The eMDMN network can be scaled up in all the schools in India under Mid-day meal scheme deploying a strong network of human resource in district and state during the project cycle. It can be further expanded into big data architecture system with cloud servers, high quality analytics, and real time information dashboards to provide focused contextual information for improving last mile delivery.

Resources required in achieving the expected results

The ministry of MHRD can join hands with any of the top technology service providers in country like TCS, Infosys, Wiproetc for high quality technical assistance and implementation support.

Partnerships

The MHRD can partner U.N. organizations like UNICEF, UNDP, and USAID for technical and financial sharing.

Figure 23: Digital system for program governance and system strengthening

Digital Governance : Connecting first through last mile

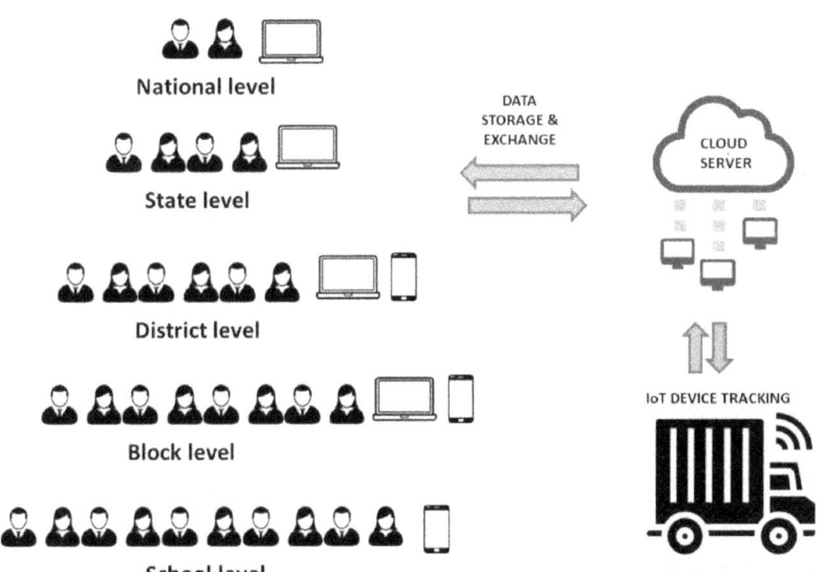

BIBLIOGRAPHY

Afridi, F. (2011). *Impact of school meals on school participation in rural India'*, Journal of Development Studies 47.11:1,1,636-56.

Retrieved:https://www.tandfonline.com/doi/abs/10.1080/00220388.2010.514330

Akshaya Patra Foundation. (2010), *PPP model best suited for implementation of Mid Day meals.* Retrieved:https://blog.akshayapatra.org/ppp-model-best-suited-for-implementing-mid-day-meals-2/

Agarwal, O.P and Somnathan, T.V.(2005).*Public Policy making in India: Issues and remedies.* Retrieved:http://www1.ximb.ac.in/users/fac/shambu/sprasad.nsf/0/e78490ff090249d06525730c0030abf9/$FILE/Public_Policy_Making_in_India_TV_SOMANATHAN.pdf

Agranoff.,R. (2003). *Leveraging networks: A guide for public managers working across organisations.* Washington, DC: IBM Endowment for the Business of Government, Retrieved:https://www.businessofgovernment.org/sites/default/files/LeveragingNetworks.pdf

Aiya,Y,et,al.(2013).*PAISA District Survey, New Delhi*: Accountability Initiative. Retrieved:https://accountabilityindia.in/blog/the-paisa-district-surveys/

Alberto, A and Igor,M. (2011). *Managing cooperation programs in developing countries: a case comparative analysis in Kenya, Pakistan, Brazil, Somalia and Egypt'* Faculty of Economics, University ofCagliari.

Retrieved:https://www.academia.edu/3059465/Managing_cooperation_programs_in_developing_countries_a_case_comparative_analysis_in_Kenya_Pakistan_Brazil_So

Ayyar,R and Vaidnatha,V. (2009). *Public Making in India'* book publishes by Dorling Kindersley (India) ISBN:9788131710272

Smith, and Gail, B. (2008). *Developing Sustainable Food Supply Chains, Philosophical Transaction: Biological Sciences*, Vol.363,No.1492, Sustainable Agriculture II, pp.849-861 Published by: The Royal Society Stable

Berry,D. Towill, R. and Wadsley, N.(1994). Supply Chain Management the Electronics Product Industry. International Journal of Physics Distribution &Logistics Management, Vol.24 No.10 ,pp. 20-32

'Capital's MCD schools mid day meal scheme fails nutrition test', Zee News.india.com, 23 May 2013

Carolyn, J and Laurence, Jr.(2005). I*s Hierarchical Governance in Decline? Evidence from Empirical Research*, Journal pf public Administration Research and Theory, Vol.15,no.2@ Journal of Public Administration Research and Theory

Chhetri, Vivek. (2006), Scam shadow on meal scheme, The Telegraph. Retrieved:https://www.telegraphindia.com/west-bengal/scam-shadow-on-meal-scheme/cid/760805

Carlsson, L and.Sandstrom, A. (2008). *Network governance of the commons*, International Journal of the Commons, Vol 2,pp-33-54

Retrieved: https://www.thecommonsjournal.org/articles/abstract/10.18352/ijc.20/

Chopra,S.and Meindle,P.(2001).*Supply Chain Management*, Prentice Hall,NJ,

Retrieved: https://base-logistique-services.com/storage/app/media/Chopra_Meindl_SCM.pdf

Comptroller and Auditor General,(2008). *Performance Audit report,* India

Retrieved: https://cag.gov.in/en/audit-report

Comptroller and Auditor General,(2007). *Performance Audit report-UP'*, India.

Retrieved:https://cag.gov.in/en/old-audit-reports?page=33

Cnristopher,M. (1994). *Logistics and Supply Chain Management,* Pitman Publishing, New York,NY

DARG. (2012). *Pilot study on Mid Day meal scheme in Dungarpur district of Rajasthan'*

Retrieved:https://mdm.cg.nic.in/Downloads/MDMChattisgarhFinalReport.pdf

Deaton, Angus and Dreze Jean.(2002). *Poverty and Inequality in India,* Economic and Political Weekly,37(36): 3729-3748 Retrieved:https://rpds.princeton.edu/sites/g/files/toruqf1956/files/media/deaton_dreze_poverty_india.pdf

Denis, Benn. (2009). *Ethics, social capital and governance: implication for public policy,* Social and Economics studies, Vol.58, No.1, Special Issue in honour of Edwin Jones, pp.141-152 Retrieved:https://uwi.edu/salises-mona/sites/salises-mona/files/PDF/AuthorIndexupto2018.pdf

Department–related Parliamentary standing Committee. (2016-17). 280 reports on the Demands for Grants, on Human Resources Development presented in Rajya Sabha.

Retrieved:http://164.100.47.5/newcommittee/reports/EnglishCommittees/Committee20HRD/280.pdf

Dhananjayan, (2003). *Origin and Growth of Nutritious Noon Meal Programme in Tamil Nadu.* Journal of India School of Political Economy, 46:55

Retrieved:https://www.worldwidejournals.com/paripex/recent_issues_pdf/2014/February/February_2014_1392717905_0c336_44.pdf

Dreze,Jean and Kingdon,G. (2001).*School Participation in Rural India.* Review of Development Economics, 5(1): 1-24.

Retrieved:https://econpapers.repec.org/article/blardevec/v_3a5_3ay_3a2001_3ai_3a1_3ap_3a1-24.htm

Drucher,P.F (1998).*Practice of Management.* Journal for East European Management Studies, Butterworth Hwinemann, Oxford,

Retrieved:https://www.econstor.eu/bitstream/10419/90303/1/773159398.pdf

Edward, A. and Daniel,L. (2002).*Public Policy and Global Supply Chain Capability and Performance: A Resource-Based View.* Journal of International Marketing, Vol.10, No.1,pp. 25-51.Sage publications,Inc.

Retrieved:https://www.jstor.org/stable/25048877

Farley,G..(1997).*Discovering Supply Chain Management: a routable discussion,* APICS- The performance Advantage, Vol.7 No.1, pp.38-9, Lion Heart Publishig,Inc.

Retrieved:https://www.lionhrtpub.com/apics/apics-1-97/Discovering.html

Fernie,John and Clive Rees.(1995).*Supply Chain Management in the national health service.* The International Journal of Logistics management, Vol.6 No.2,pp.83-92

Retrieved:https://www.scribd.com/document/135851028/InTech-Supply-Chain-Management-Scm-Theory-and-Evolution#

Government of India,(2011).Mid Day Meal Scheme. Retrieved:https://pmposhan.education.gov.in/Meal%20Provision.html

Shanmugam, K . et.al,.(2012).*Performance of Flagship Programmes in Tamil Nadu* Madras School of Economics.

Retrieved:https://www.mse.ac.in/wp-content/uploads/2021/05/monograph-18.pdf

Khera,R. (2006). *Mid Day Meals in Primary Schools: Achievement and Challenges.* Economic and Political Weekly, 41(46), 4742-50.

Retrieved:https://www.jstor.org/stable/4418915

Kaushal, Savita.(2009). A *Study of Best practices in the implementation of Mid Day Meal programme in Rajasthan'*,NUEPA,New Delhi

Retrieved:http://mdm.nic.in/Mid-day-meal-best-practices-by-savita-kaushal-nuepa.pdf

Kadari,R&Roy,S. (2016). *Strengthening the MDMS through MIS and IVRS in Utter Pradesh.* ISBN No-2454-9614, South Asian Journal of Engineering and Technology Vol 2,No-10 pg 1-9.

Retrieved: http://citeseerx.ist.psu.edu/viewdoc/download pdf

LauranceJ,O'.Toole Jr.(2001). *Research on Policy Implementation: Assessment and Prospects.* oxford Journals Social Sciences Jnl. of Public Admin. Research and Theory Volume 10, Issue 2pp.263-288

Lu,Dawel. (2011). *Fundamental of Supply Chain management.* Ventus publishing Aps,ISBN 978-87-7681-798-5

Madhaiyan, R.(2014). I*ndia's Hunger Problem: A comparative analysis of the performance of food distribution at the national level and in the state of Tamil Nadu.* Master thesis in Sustainable Development at Uppsala University, No. 178,30pp

Retrieved:http://www.diva-portal.org/smash/get/diva2:691074/FULLTEXT01.pdf

Mathur,Kuldeep.(2001).*Governance and alternative sources of policy advice: the case of India.'* in K,Weaver and Paul Stares (eds),Guidance for Governance, Japan Centre for International Exchange and Brookings Institute.

Manus,J.(2008). *A governance perspectives. European Institute of Economic development.* Researchgate,ERDU, University of Lincoln UK.

Retrieved:https://www.researchgate.net/publication/279426357_A_governance_perspective

Meena,S.(2010). *Impact of Noon Meal programme on Primary Education: An Exploratory study in Tamil Nadu.* Economic and Political Weekly,23,pp24-26

Retrieved:https://www.worldwidejournals.com/paripex/recent_issues_pdf/2014/February/February_2014_1392 717905_0c336_44.pdf

Melissa,M. et,al.(2006). *Building a policy fields framework to inform research on nonprofit organization.* University of Minnesota, Public Administration Review,Vol. 66, Special Issue: Collaborative Public Management (Dec., 2006), pp. 44-55 (12 pages) Published By: Wiley

Retrieved:https://www.jstor.org/stable/4096569.

Menon,P.(2009). *Best practice adopted in mid day meal scheme case studies of 28 states including Delhi and Pondicherry.* Department of Educational Policy NUEPA, New Delhi

MHRD (2014),'report on innovative practice in MDM.'

MHRD (2011) 3rd review of Mid Day Meal programme Tamil Nadu

MHRD (2014) 5th Joint Review Mission on Mid Day Scheme Tamil Nadu

Mooij, Jos.(2000). *Food policy in India: the important of electoral politics in policy implementation.* Journal of International Development, Vol.11, pp.625-36

Pauddel,N.(2007). *A critical account of policy implementation theories: Status and reconsideration,*Vol.3,pp-9-12. Published by: Springer

PMSA Committee.(2013). *The role of evidence in policy formation and implementation.* ISBN 978-0-477-10404-3(paperback),Symonds Street, Auckland 1150,New Zealand

PEO, Planning Commission, (2010). *Performance evaluation of cooked mid day meal (CMDM),India.*

Prasad,Archana.(2013). *Mid Day Meal Scheme, Nutrition and Corporate capital.* People's Democracy (Communist party of India (Marxist).XXXVII (30)

Pratichi Trust,(2005). *Cooked mid day meal programme in West Bengal: A study in Birbhum District*

http://www.pratichi.org/wp-content/uploads/2021/04/2005 Cooked_Midday_Meal_Programme_Birbhum.pdf

Parikh, Kalpana and yasmeen,Summiya. (2010). Groundswell for Mid Day Meal Scheme.

Retrieved: http://www.indiatogether.org/cgi-bin/tools/pfriend.cgi

Rani, Anima Si and Sherma,Naresh.(2008). *An Empirical Study of the Mid Day Meal Programme in Khurda, Orissa,* Economic & Political Weekly Retrieved:https://www.academia.edu/776223/An_empirical_Study_of_ the_Mid_Day_Meal_programme_in_Khurda_Orissa

Rukmani,R. (2011). The M S Swaminathan Research Foundation has prepared the document on Indian experience with regard to school feeding.

Andrews, Rhys.et,al.(2005). *Strategy, structure and process in the public sector: A test of the miles and snow model.* Journal of Public Administration research and theory, 87(4):732 - 749

Rao,Shrilata and Ramakrishnan, Jyoti. (2017). *What do the children eat at school, Teachers' Account, Book name,' Nutritional Adequacy, Diversity and Choice among primary school children,* Policy and practice in India, published in Springer, pp 125-141

Roy, Vivek.et, al.(2017). *Supplier participation towards addressing sustainability-oriented objectives of the mid day meal supply chain.* International Journal of logistics management (Emereld) DOI:10.1108/IJLM-12-2016-0297 Retrieved https://www.researchgate.net/publication

RyuS,S. (2013). *Gender, public management and organisational performance: Evidence from Indonesian Public schools.* Presentation at the 2013 Korean Association for Public Administration's International Conferences, Seoul, Korea

Fernandez, S. (2003). *Developing and testing an integrative framework of public sector managerial leadership: evidence from the public education arena.* Paper presented at the 7th national Public management research Conference, Washington D.C

Nambiyar,S.et,al.(2010). *Innovation in Delivery of mid day meal scheme through public private partnership.* Paper submitted at the NAPSIPAG,7th International Conference, Reaching out to people: Achieving Millennium Development Goals through Innovation Public Service Delivery

Sinha, Dipa.(2008A). *Social Audit of Mid Day Meal Scheme in AP.* Economical and Political Weekly.43 (44):57-61,DOI 10.2307/40278130

Retrieved:https://www.researchgate.net/publication/261890487_Social_Audit_of_Midday_Meal_Scheine_in_AP

Sagar, P and Madan, P.(2009). *Public policy consulting in emerging Indian framework.* BerichteAus Der P4axis Vol 2,Issue 4,pp 663-677

Sindhu, A.(2014).*MID DAY MEAL WORKERS: Fighting for Rights- Relentless and Determined.* Vol XXXIX No.03, People Democracy

https://peoplesdemocracy.in/2014/0223_pd/mid-day-meal-workers-fighting-rights-%E2%80%93-relentless-and-determined

Singh, P. et,al. (2018). *Network design in Mid Day Meal programme.* Dissertation for master of applied science in supply chain management at the Massachusetts Institute of Technology

Retrieved:https://dspace.mit.edu/bitstream/handle//Noor_Singh_2018_Capstone.pdf

Sapkota.R,(2016). *Value chain analysis of Mid Day Meal Scheme in Karnataka.* Project report submitted to TERI University for master degree in sustainable development practice.

Retrieved:https://static1.squarespace.com/static/ranjita_value+chain_portfolio.pdf

Government of Tamil Nadu .(2014-2015).Department policy note on social welfare and nutritious meal programme. http://cms.tn.gov.in/sites/default/files/ documents/swnmp_e_pn_2015_16.pdf

The ISKON, a Bangalore based initiated Akshya Patra Foundation in Gujarat in 2004

United Nation (2011), The Millennium Development Goals report 2011.New York,NY,

Retrieved from: http://www.un.org/millenniumgoals/pdf/(2011_E)

Athreya,V.(2011).*The experience of the south Indian state of Tamil Nadu with school feeding programmes is instructive in many ways.* PMID: 12281938 ,DOI: 10.1016/0306-9192(89)90026-2

World Bank Document March,2020,'Policy Recharge Work Paper prospect Risk 9181'.

Retrieved from:https://documents1.worldbank.org/curated/en/787881584027048587

https://pmposhan.education.gov.in/

World Bank group, 2015, Education Global Practices

Press Trust India, Jul 26, 2013, 03.31PM IST-PATNA

Press Trust India, Jul 27, 2013, 01.38PM IST-BERHAMPUR (Odisha)

Press Trust India, Jul 20, 2013, 03.25PM IST-PANAJI

Press Trust India, Jul 21, 2013, 01.34PM IST- HIRUVANANTHAPURAM

Press Trust India, Jul 27, 2013, 01.43PM IST-BALAGHAT (Madhy Pradesh):

Priya Abraham-The Telegraph (September 3 , 2013)- Cases in Odisha

Times of India, Jul 29, 2013, 08.33PM IST-

TNN | Mar 28, 2014, 03.39 AM IST-DOMJUR Howrah

TNN | Mar 9, 2014, 02.20 AM IST-MANGALORE

TNN | Sep 19, 2013, 01.25 AM IST-BHOPAL (Madhy Pradesh)

www.reutersreprints.com.

www.righttofoodindia.org/data

Retrieved from:http://www.telegraphindia.com/1061115/asp/siliguri/story_7001871

Retrieved fromhttp://india.gov.in/sectors/education/index.php?id=7. 30

http://pmindia.nic.in/nac/communication/meal.pdf

http://www.ifpri.org/ghi/2012

http://www.mssrf.org/sites/default/files/School-Feeding-Programmes-in-India.pdf

http://www.tn.gov.in/documents/search/mid%20day%20meal

indiabudget.nic.in/ub2013-14/bh/bh1.pdf

www.Oracle.com